PAT BROWN, MBA

GolfMoney101

Using Golf to Teach the Basics of Money

ABRAM · 47 · BROWN

First published by AbramBrown47 2026

First edition

ISBN: 978-1-967737-64-2

This book was professionally typeset on Reedsy.
Find out more at reedsy.com

Contents

Foreword v
Introduction viii
About This Book xi
Foolish Assumptions xiv
How This Playbook Is Organized xvii
About Pat Brown xx
Part I: Grip, Stance, and Fundamentals 1
Chapter 1: Why Money Feels Confusing After Golf 4
Chapter 2: Read the Scorecard: Your Financial Snapshot 8
Chapter 3: Eliminating Penalty Strokes: Budgeting and Saving 13
Chapter 4: Credit, Debt, and Hazard Shots 18
Chapter 5: The Golf Bag of Money: Banking Basics 23
Part II: Course Management, Defense, and Protection 28
Chapter 6: Risk Awareness and Shot Selection 31
Chapter 7: Insurance Fundamentals Every Player Needs 35
Chapter 8: Life, Disability, and Liability Protection 40
Part III: Constructing the Shot (Investing Fundamentals) 44
Chapter 9: How Financial Markets Really Work 46
Chapter 10: Risk, Return, and the Power of Compounding 51
Chapter 11: Stocks Without the Highlight Swing 56
Chapter 12: Bonds and Playing the Long Fairway 61
Chapter 13: Funds, ETFs, and Team Golf Investing 66
Chapter 14: Real Estate and Alternative Courses 71
Part IV: Managing the Round 76
Chapter 15: Asset Allocation and Course Positioning 78
Chapter 16: Buying, Holding, and Trusting Your Swing 83

Chapter 17: Rebalancing and Momentum Shifts 88
Chapter 18: The Mental Side of Money 93
Part V: The Long Season and Life Beyond the Course 98
Chapter 19: Taxes and Where You Place Your Shots 101
Chapter 20: Retirement Accounts and Financial Independence 106
Chapter 21: Housing and Major Financial Decisions 111
Chapter 22: Your Career Is Your Longest Round 116
Chapter 23: Estate Planning Basics Everyone Needs 121
Chapter 24: Talking About Money With Family 126
Part VI: Winning the Match Over Time 131
Chapter 25: Advisors, Scams, and Long-Term Success 134
Chapter 26: Losing the Schedule and Rebuilding Structure 138
Chapter 27: From Teammates to Coworkers 144
Chapter 28: When No One Is Watching Anymore 150
Chapter 29: Redefining Winning After the Uniform Comes Off 156
Chapter 30: Staying Connected Without Living in the Past 162
Disclaimers 168
Glossary of Golf and Financial Terms 171

Foreword

Golf has a way of revealing who you are.

It does not care about reputation, past success, or what you shot last week. Every round starts the same way. One ball. One club. One decision at a time. You cannot fake it for eighteen holes. The course will expose impatience, poor preparation, and emotional decision-making faster than almost anything else.

Money works the same way.

I have watched countless talented, disciplined, hardworking athletes struggle financially, not because they lacked ability, but because they never learned how to play the financial version of the game. They trained for years to master their sport, yet were handed real money with no instruction manual, no coach, and no clear strategy. They were expected to figure it out on the fly while pressure and noise surrounded them.

That is not a fair fight.

GolfMoney101 exists because the lessons that make great golfers are the same lessons that build long-term financial success. Patience. Discipline. Fundamentals. Course management. Emotional control. Trusting the process even when the results are not immediate.

In golf, nobody expects a beginner to walk onto a championship course and shoot a low score without learning the basics. Grip comes before shot shaping. Tempo comes before distance. Strategy comes before aggression. Yet financially, people are often expected to make high-stakes decisions without understanding the basics of how money works.

This book closes that gap.

What makes this approach powerful is that it speaks the language athletes already understand. You do not need complex formulas or financial jargon to make smart money decisions. You need a framework that mirrors how you already think about preparation, performance, and long-term development. Golf provides that framework naturally.

Every golfer has faced moments where emotion threatens to take over. A bad bounce. A missed putt. A double bogey that feels unfair. The golfers who succeed are not the ones who never make mistakes. They are the ones who respond well. They reset. They stick to their plan. They do not let one bad hole ruin the round.

Financial setbacks are no different.

Unexpected expenses happen. Markets fluctuate. Careers change. Income rises and falls. The people who win financially are not the ones who avoid adversity. They are the ones who have systems in place that allow them to stay composed and make smart decisions under pressure.

This book does not promise shortcuts. It does not sell hype. It does not pretend that money is easy or that every decision will work out perfectly. What it offers is something far more valuable. A clear, repeatable approach to managing money the same way successful athletes manage their sport.

Pat Brown writes from lived experience. As a former athlete and a financial professional, he understands both sides of the equation. He understands the mindset athletes bring to competition and the blind spots that often come with it. More importantly, he understands how to translate discipline from the course into real-world financial behavior that lasts long after the final round.

This book respects the reader. It assumes effort. It assumes competitiveness. It assumes a willingness to learn and improve. It does not talk down to athletes or oversimplify the stakes. Instead, it reframes money as another arena where preparation and consistency matter more than talent or luck.

GolfMoney101 is not about becoming obsessed with money. It is about removing stress, uncertainty, and confusion so you can focus on what matters most. It is about building confidence through understanding, not through risk-taking or speculation. It is about learning when to be aggressive and when to stay patient.

Most importantly, it is about playing the long game.

Golf teaches that championships are not won with one perfect shot. They are won by stacking good decisions, avoiding big mistakes, and staying mentally strong over time. Financial success follows the same path.

If you commit to the principles in this book the same way you commit to your training, the results will show up. Not overnight, but steadily. Quietly. Reliably.

That is how real winners are built.

Introduction

You Win Tournaments One Shot at a Time

Every golfer knows this feeling.

You step onto the first tee. The course looks long. The wind is up. The scorecard feels intimidating. Maybe you had a great range session. Maybe you didn't. Either way, the round is about to start, and none of that matters anymore.

You do not win a tournament on the first hole.

You do not lose it there either.

You win tournaments one shot at a time.

Golf teaches patience in a way few sports do. You can do everything right on a swing and still end up in a bunker. You can hit a bad shot and get a good bounce. Over eighteen holes, luck shows up, but discipline decides the outcome. The players who stay composed, trust their fundamentals, and avoid big mistakes are the ones still standing on Sunday afternoon.

Money works the exact same way.

Most athletes and golfers struggle with money not because they are irresponsible, but because no one ever taught them how to play the long round. Financial decisions come fast, feel emotional, and often happen without a clear plan. One bad decision can feel like a triple bogey that wrecks your confidence. One lucky break can create false confidence that leads to even bigger mistakes later.

This book is about helping you stop forcing shots you do not need to hit.

In golf, you learn quickly that trying to hit a miracle shot through trees usually makes things worse. Smart golfers take their medicine. They punch out, get back in position, and give themselves a chance on the next hole. Financially, the same rule applies. The goal is not to look impressive in the moment. The goal is to put yourself in position over time.

Golf rewards players who respect fundamentals. Grip, stance, alignment, tempo. None of those are flashy, but every great player obsesses over them. Money has its own version of fundamentals. Understanding cash flow. Managing risk. Protecting against disaster. Investing with discipline. Avoiding emotional decisions when pressure is high.

If you skip the basics, everything else breaks down.

Many athletes approach money the way amateurs approach golf. They chase distance before learning control. They buy equipment instead of fixing mechanics. They listen to whoever sounds confident instead of trusting proven fundamentals. In money, that shows up as chasing hot investments, copying what others are doing, or taking advice from people who have never played the long game themselves.

Golf punishes that behavior over time.

This book is written for athletes and competitors who understand preparation, reps, coaching, and accountability. You already know what it means to train when no one is watching. You know that consistency beats intensity. You know that the scoreboard does not care about excuses. Those same lessons apply directly to your financial life.

You do not need to become a finance expert to win with money. You need a repeatable system. You need to understand when to attack and when to lay up. You need to protect yourself from blow-up holes. You need to trust the process even when the round feels slow.

Some readers may be student-athletes just starting to earn money. Others may be former players navigating life after the game. Some may experience sudden income or opportunities that feel overwhelming. No matter where you are in the journey, the principles do not change. Golf does not care who you are or how you got there. Money does not either.

This book is not about shortcuts. It is about playing smart golf with your finances. It is about stacking good decisions the same way you stack pars. It is about understanding that championships are not won with one heroic swing, but with hundreds of disciplined shots taken the right way.

You win tournaments one shot at a time.

You win financially the exact same way.

About This Book

Golf is a game of preparation, patience, and honesty.

There are no shortcuts. You cannot rush improvement. You cannot hide mistakes. The ball does not care how confident you feel or how badly you want a good result. It responds only to what you do. Over time, golfers learn that success comes from fundamentals, discipline, and smart decision-making, not from forcing outcomes.

Money works the exact same way.

This book exists to show how the lessons golfers already understand can be applied directly to financial life. You do not need to relearn how to think. You simply need to apply familiar principles to a different arena. Golf provides a natural framework for understanding money because both require long-term thinking, emotional control, and consistent execution.

In golf, every round is a series of decisions. Club selection. Shot shape. Target choice. Risk assessment. You are constantly weighing upside against downside. Should you go for the green or lay up? Should you attack the pin or play to the center? These decisions rarely feel dramatic in isolation, but they add up over time. The same is true financially. Small decisions about spending, saving, investing, and protecting yourself compound into meaningful outcomes.

One of the most important lessons golf teaches is that avoiding big mistakes matters more than chasing perfection. A round can survive a missed putt. It rarely survives repeated penalty strokes. Financially, this shows up in avoiding high-interest debt, protecting against major risks, and resisting emotional decisions. You do not need to hit every shot perfectly to succeed with money. You need to stay out of trouble.

Golf also teaches humility. Even the best players hit bad shots. Conditions change. Variables exist outside your control. The difference between amateurs and professionals is not that professionals avoid mistakes. It is that they respond better. They accept the result, make the next smart decision, and move on. Money demands the same mindset. Markets fluctuate. Life happens. Plans need adjustments. The ability to stay composed matters more than being right all the time.

This book is written for athletes and competitors who understand structure and accountability. You know what it means to practice with purpose. You know that progress often feels slow before it becomes visible. You know that discipline shows up long before results do. Those lessons transfer directly to financial success.

Golf teaches that fundamentals come first. Grip, stance, alignment, and tempo are non-negotiable. Without them, advanced techniques fall apart. Money has its own fundamentals. Understanding cash flow. Managing risk. Protecting your income. Investing with patience. This book starts with those basics because everything else depends on them.

Another core lesson golf teaches is personal responsibility. There is no one else to blame for a bad swing. You own the result. Financial decisions carry the same weight. Outsourcing responsibility, ignoring statements, or blindly trusting others does not remove accountability. This book emphasizes understanding enough to ask good questions and make informed decisions, even if you work with professionals.

This book does not assume you want to become obsessed with money. It assumes you want clarity. Confidence. Control. The goal is not to turn finances into a constant source of stress. The goal is to build systems that run in the background, allowing you to focus on your career, family, and life beyond the course.

GolfMoney101 is not about winning one hole. It is about managing the entire round. It is about knowing when to be aggressive and when to stay patient. It is about trusting a process that works even when conditions are challenging.

If you approach money the same way you approach golf practice, improvement is inevitable. Show up consistently. Respect fundamentals. Make smart decisions. Accept setbacks without panic. Over time, the results will take care of themselves.

Golf teaches us that success is rarely loud. It is built quietly, one shot at a time.

Foolish Assumptions

Every good coach starts with assumptions.

Some are fair. Some are optimistic. Some are probably wrong. But coaches make them anyway, because teaching requires a baseline. This section is honest about the assumptions behind this book so you know exactly who it is written for and who it is not written for.

The first assumption is that you are competitive.

You do not have to be a professional golfer or a scratch player, but you have competed at something that mattered to you. You understand preparation. You understand pressure. You understand the difference between going through the motions and actually committing to improvement. This book assumes you care about getting better, even when the process is uncomfortable or slow.

The second assumption is that you are coachable.

That does not mean you blindly follow instructions. It means you are willing to listen, test ideas, and adjust when something is not working. Golfers who refuse to change their grip or alignment rarely improve. Financially, the same stubbornness shows up when people cling to habits that are hurting them. This book assumes you are open to feedback and willing to make small changes that add up over time.

The third assumption is that you respect fundamentals.

Golf rewards players who master the basics before chasing advanced techniques. This book assumes you are willing to start there financially. Understanding cash flow, risk, and protection may not feel exciting, but skipping them leads to inconsistency and stress. If you are looking for shortcuts, secrets, or guaranteed outcomes, this book will probably frustrate you.

Another assumption is that you value long-term success over short-term appearance.

In golf, chasing distance at the expense of control leads to higher scores. Financially, chasing quick wins or flashy opportunities often creates regret. This book assumes you would rather build something sustainable than impress people in the moment. It assumes you are willing to make decisions that may look boring now but pay off later.

This book also assumes you are human.

You will make mistakes. You will have emotional reactions. You will sometimes want to swing harder when patience is required. Golfers do this all the time. Financial decisions are no different. This book does not assume perfection. It assumes awareness. It assumes you are willing to acknowledge errors, reset, and make the next smart decision instead of spiraling.

Another assumption is that you want ownership, not excuses.

Golf does not allow much finger-pointing. Weather, course conditions, and bad breaks happen, but your response still matters. Financially, blaming the system, the market, or other people may feel justified, but it does not improve outcomes. This book assumes you want control over what you can control and are willing to take responsibility for your decisions.

This book also assumes you want clarity, not complexity.

Golf instruction that overcomplicates the swing usually does more harm than good. Financial education works the same way. This book avoids unnecessary jargon and technical overload. The goal is understanding, not intimidation. If something feels confusing, the problem is not you. It is the explanation.

One more assumption is that you are willing to be patient.

Golf improvement is not linear. Neither is financial progress. There will be stretches where it feels like nothing is happening. This book assumes you understand that progress often shows up quietly and that staying disciplined during slow periods is part of winning the long game.

Finally, this book assumes you want your money to support your life, not control it.

Golf is a game, but life is bigger than the course. Money should be a tool that creates options, not a source of constant stress or distraction. This book assumes you want confidence and freedom, not obsession.

If any of these assumptions feel uncomfortable, that is not a bad thing. Good coaching often starts with discomfort. The goal is not to judge. The goal is to set expectations clearly so the work can begin.

These assumptions may be foolish. Or they may be exactly what you need to hear.

How This Playbook Is Organized

This book is organized the same way a smart golfer approaches improvement and competition.

You do not start by trying to hit miracle shots. You start by building a foundation that holds up under pressure. You learn the basics, then layer in strategy, protection, and decision-making. Over time, those pieces come together into a repeatable system you can trust on any course, in any conditions.

That structure is intentional.

GolfMoney101 is divided into parts that mirror how golfers actually develop and how successful financial lives are built.

The early sections focus on fundamentals. In golf, grip, stance, and alignment come before shot shaping or course strategy. Financially, this means understanding how money flows in and out of your life, how to avoid unnecessary penalties, and how to protect yourself from common mistakes. Without these basics, everything else becomes unstable.

The next sections move into course management and defense. Good golfers do not just think about how to score. They think about how to avoid disaster. They respect hazards, understand risk, and choose shots that keep them in position. In this book, that translates to insurance, risk awareness, and protecting your income and assets. These chapters are about staying in the tournament even when things do not go perfectly.

From there, the book shifts into investing fundamentals. This is where many people want to start, but starting here without a base often leads to frustration. Investing is like shot construction. You need to understand how the club works, how conditions affect outcomes, and why consistency beats hero swings. These chapters explain markets, risk, diversification, and long-term strategy using golf concepts that make the ideas easier to understand and apply.

Once the basics of investing are in place, the book moves into managing the round. Even great plans require adjustments. Wind changes. Lies are uneven. Momentum shifts. These chapters focus on asset allocation, buying and holding, rebalancing, and the mental side of money. The goal is not constant tweaking. The goal is knowing when to adjust and when to trust your swing.

The later sections focus on the long season and life beyond the course. Golf careers change. Bodies change. Priorities shift. Financially, this is where taxes, retirement, housing, career decisions, and family conversations come into play. These chapters acknowledge that money decisions do not happen in isolation. They happen alongside life events, responsibilities, and transitions.

The final part brings everything together. Winning financially is not about avoiding advisors or doing everything alone. It is about knowing when to ask for help, how to recognize bad advice, and how to stay focused on long-term success. This section reinforces the idea that smart money management is a lifelong process, not a one-time decision.

Each chapter is written to stand on its own while still fitting into the bigger picture. You do not need to read this book in one sitting. Just like golf practice, progress comes from consistent reps. Some chapters may feel immediately relevant. Others may matter more later. That is normal.

This playbook is not meant to overwhelm you. It is meant to give you a framework you can return to when decisions feel confusing or stressful. Just like a pre-shot routine, structure creates calm. When you know the process, you are less likely to panic or force decisions.

You will notice that this book avoids hype and guarantees. Golf does not promise perfect rounds. Money does not promise perfect outcomes. What both can offer is improvement through discipline, preparation, and smart decision-making over time.

Think of this book as a caddie, not a commentator. It is here to help you see the course clearly, choose smart shots, and stay composed when pressure builds. You still have to swing the club. You still have to make the decisions. The value comes from understanding the course you are playing.

If you follow the structure of this playbook the same way you follow a training plan, the results will show up. Quietly. Consistently. One smart decision at a time.

About Pat Brown

Pat Brown's approach to money, discipline, and long-term thinking was shaped long before he ever worked in financial services. It was built in locker rooms, weight rooms, and meeting rooms where accountability was not optional and preparation was expected.

Pat played college football at the University of Kansas from 1994 to 1999 and was named team captain for the 1999 season. Those years taught him lessons that extend far beyond sports. Football demanded consistency, attention to detail, and responsibility to the team. Showing up prepared, doing your job, and leading by example were not slogans, they were expectations. Those same principles continue to guide Pat's work today.

Following his playing career, Pat transitioned into financial services and built a career as a financial advisor and wealth manager. He works with individuals, families, business owners, and athletes navigating increasingly complex financial decisions. Over time, he noticed a familiar pattern. People who were disciplined and successful in one area of life often struggled with money simply because they were never taught how to manage it.

To strengthen his foundation, Pat pursued advanced education and professional development. He earned an MBA and completed multiple industry designations, including the Chartered Financial Consultant designation, the Retirement Income Certified Professional designation, and the Chartered Advisor in Philanthropy designation. His background blends academic training with real-world experience in financial planning, retirement income strategies, tax planning, and charitable giving.

As the college sports landscape changed with the introduction of Name, Image, and Likeness opportunities, Pat recognized a growing education gap.

Student athletes were gaining access to income, contracts, and endorsements without the financial knowledge needed to handle taxes, cash flow, business structures, and long-term consequences. Many were expected to make adult financial decisions with little guidance while balancing athletics, academics, and personal development.

That reality became a turning point in Pat's work.

He shifted much of his focus toward athlete financial education, particularly in the NIL space. His goal was not to complicate money, but to make it understandable and actionable. He emphasized fundamentals, structure, and long-term thinking over hype or shortcuts.

Pat has since become a recognized voice in athlete financial education and has been interviewed by national publications and platforms including Financial Planning, Yahoo, and ESPN Andscape. In these conversations, he consistently highlights the need for early financial education and the risks athletes face when opportunity arrives before understanding.

These experiences led Pat to author a series of practical, athlete-focused books designed to meet athletes and families where they are. His NIL-related titles include Financial Literacy for NIL, Financial Literacy for NIL for Parents of Student Athletes, Financial Literacy for NIL for High School Students, and Financial Literacy for NIL for International Student Athletes. Each book is written to be clear, accessible, and grounded in real-world scenarios.

Pat also created a growing collection of sport-specific financial education books, including Football Money 101, Baseball Money 101, Basketball Money 101, Cheer Money 101, Dance Money 101, Gymnastics Money 101, Hockey Money 101, Lacrosse Money 101, Rowing Money 101, Soccer Money 101, Softball Money 101, Tennis Money 101, Track Money 101, Volleyball Money 101, Wrestling Money 101, and GolfMoney101. Each title translates the culture, discipline, and mindset of the sport into financial lessons that last long after competition ends.

To extend this work beyond books, Pat founded Former Student Athlete, a platform created to support athletes navigating life after sports. Former Student Athlete provides education, community, and real-world resources focused on financial literacy, career transitions, health, identity, and long-term success once the uniform comes off. More information can be found at www.formerstudentathlete.com, www.financialliteracyfornil.com, and www.financialliteracyforstudentathletes.com.

Pat is active online through professional platforms and social media, where he regularly shares insights on athletes, money, and life after sports. If you would like to connect with Pat specifically about GolfMoney101, he can be reached directly at info@golfmoney101.com.

At the core of Pat's work is a belief shaped by both sports and finance. Athletes deserve a better playbook for life beyond competition, and financial education should arrive before opportunity turns into regret.

Part I: Grip, Stance, and Fundamentals

You cannot play great golf without mastering the basics.

Every golfer wants to hit great shots.

Most golfers skip the part that makes great shots possible.

Grip, stance, posture, alignment, and tempo are not exciting. They do not show up on highlight reels. They are rarely talked about once a player advances past the beginner stage. Yet every elite golfer, regardless of style or personality, revisits these fundamentals constantly. When things go wrong, they do not look for tricks. They go back to the basics.

Money works the same way.

Most financial stress comes from ignoring or misunderstanding fundamentals. People want to talk about investing strategies, market predictions, and big opportunities before they understand how money actually moves through their lives. That is like trying to shape shots without knowing where the clubface is pointing. You might get lucky for a while, but eventually the inconsistency shows up.

This section of the book is intentionally unglamorous.

It focuses on the financial equivalents of grip, stance, and setup. These chapters are about how money comes in, how it goes out, how to avoid unnecessary penalties, and how to create stability before chasing performance. Without these pieces in place, even good investment decisions can fail because the foundation is shaky.

In golf, a poor grip affects every swing. It does not matter how athletic you are or how strong you feel. If the club is not in your hands correctly, you will fight the ball all day. Financially, poor cash flow management does the same thing. You can earn good money and still feel constantly behind if you do not understand where it is going.

Stance and alignment matter because they determine where the ball starts. Many golfers aim poorly without realizing it, then spend the round trying to fix a problem that was created before the swing even started. Financial mistakes often work the same way. Decisions made early, like lifestyle choices, debt habits, or lack of savings, quietly push everything off line. Later decisions feel harder than they need to be because the setup was wrong.

Fundamentals also create confidence.

Golfers who trust their setup swing more freely. They do not manipulate the club mid-swing. They let the motion happen. Financial confidence comes from knowing you have structure. Emergency savings. A plan for bills. Protection against common risks. When those pieces exist, decisions feel calmer and less emotional.

This part of the book addresses why money often feels confusing for athletes, how to take an honest financial snapshot, how to eliminate penalty strokes like unnecessary debt, and how basic banking actually works. None of this is complicated, but it does require attention and honesty. Just like golf, ignoring fundamentals does not make them go away.

Another reason fundamentals matter is durability.

In golf, fundamentals hold up under pressure. When nerves show up, muscle memory takes over. Financial pressure works the same way. Unexpected expenses, income changes, or life transitions test your systems. If the basics are solid, you bend without breaking. If they are not, stress compounds quickly.

Athletes often underestimate how much their sports mindset already prepares them for this work. You understand repetition. You understand delayed gratification. You understand that improvement comes from doing simple things consistently, not from chasing shortcuts. This section simply translates those instincts into financial behavior.

Think of Part I as your financial setup routine.

It may not feel exciting, but it determines everything that follows. Great rounds are built before the first swing. Great financial outcomes are built before the first investment.

If you commit to mastering these basics, the rest of the book becomes easier to apply. Just like golf, once the foundation is solid, you can play with confidence, creativity, and control.

Chapter 1: Why Money Feels Confusing After Golf

Golf teaches structure. Money usually does not.

A golfer can spend years learning fundamentals before ever playing a serious round. Grip, stance, alignment, tempo, course management. Every step is coached, corrected, and reinforced. Feedback is constant. Results are visible. Improvement, while slow, makes sense.

Money shows up very differently.

For many athletes and golfers, money arrives without instruction. There is no practice range. No coach standing behind you fixing your setup. No scorecard that clearly explains why things went wrong. One day you are focused on training, competition, and performance. The next day you are expected to manage income, expenses, taxes, savings, and investments with little guidance.

That gap is where confusion begins.

Why financial literacy is rarely taught to athletes

Most athletic systems are designed to produce performance, not education outside the sport. Clubs, academies, high school programs, college teams, and even professional environments focus on skill development, conditioning, and results. Financial education is often viewed as someone else's responsibility or something that can wait.

The problem is that money does not wait.

Athletes often earn money earlier than their peers. Lessons, tournaments, stipends, prize money, sponsorships, or NIL income can arrive before adulthood. Yet very few programs teach how to manage that income responsibly. The assumption is that someone else will step in later, or that earning more money will somehow solve the problem.

Golf does not work that way.

More distance does not fix bad alignment. More money does not fix bad habits.

When financial education is missing, athletes rely on informal sources. Teammates. Coaches. Parents. Social media. These sources may be well intentioned, but they are rarely consistent or accurate. Over time, this creates a patchwork understanding of money that feels confusing and unreliable.

Money myths passed through clubs, academies, and locker rooms

Every locker room has money myths.

Some sound confident. Some sound motivational. Most are incomplete or wrong.

You hear things like save later, invest early and aggressively, real estate is always safe, or just find a hot stock. These ideas spread the same way swing tips do from unqualified sources. One person had a good experience, tells the story confidently, and suddenly it becomes advice.

In golf, this creates bad habits quickly. One player suggests a grip change that worked for them. Another copies it without understanding why. Results get worse, not better. Money myths do the same thing. Advice without context leads to decisions without structure.

Another common myth is that smart people automatically figure money out. Golf disproves that idea easily. Intelligence does not replace fundamentals. Financial success requires education and repetition, not just confidence.

Athletes are also exposed to survivorship bias. You hear about the one person who took a big risk and won. You do not hear about the many who tried the same thing and failed quietly. Golfers understand this instinctively. You see the highlight shot on television, not the dozens of poor decisions that never made it to the broadcast.

Saving vs investing vs gambling

One major source of confusion is the difference between saving, investing, and gambling.

Saving is about protection and flexibility. It is the financial equivalent of laying up to a safe distance. Emergency funds, short-term goals, and cash reserves are not meant to impress. They are meant to keep you in the round.

Investing is about long-term growth. It is like playing a smart approach shot over many holes. There will be ups and downs, but the goal is steady progress over time. Investing relies on patience, discipline, and consistency.

Gambling is about outcomes without control. It feels exciting. It promises quick results. It ignores process. In golf terms, it is the forced hero shot through trees when a punch-out would do.

Many athletes confuse these categories because no one explains the difference clearly. Money put into the market for short-term needs is not investing. It is risk-taking. Chasing tips, trends, or hype without understanding risk is not investing. It is gambling.

Golfers understand this distinction on the course. You choose shots based on distance, lie, conditions, and score. Money decisions require the same discipline.

Why consistency beats chasing miracle shots

Golf punishes impatience.

Trying to win a round with miracle shots usually leads to penalty strokes. Smart golfers accept that pars win tournaments. They focus on fairways, greens, and avoiding big numbers. Over time, consistency creates scoring opportunities.

Financial success works the same way.

Consistent saving, steady investing, and disciplined decision-making outperform flashy strategies over time. Chasing big wins often leads to setbacks that are hard to recover from. The damage is not always immediate, but it compounds quietly.

Athletes are wired to compete and push limits. That mindset is powerful when paired with structure. Without structure, it creates risk. Money rewards those who stay patient, follow a plan, and avoid emotional swings.

The reason money feels confusing after golf is not because it is more complex. It is because the structure is missing. Once you apply the same principles you already understand from the course, money becomes clearer and more manageable.

This chapter is about recognizing that the confusion is not a personal failure. It is a coaching gap. And like any gap, it can be closed with the right fundamentals.

Athlete Takeaways

- Money needs coaching the same way your golf swing did
- Advice without fundamentals creates bad habits fast
- Saving protects your round, investing builds your score, gambling blows it up
- Chasing miracle shots works on TV, not over a full season
- Consistency and discipline beat hype every time

Chapter 2: Read the Scorecard: Your Financial Snapshot

Every golfer learns early that the scorecard matters, even when it is uncomfortable.

You might feel like you are playing well. The swing feels smooth. Contact sounds clean. But the scorecard does not care how it feels. It records what actually happened. Fair or unfair, lucky or unlucky, the number is the number. Golfers who refuse to look at the scorecard usually make worse decisions as the round goes on because they lose context.

Money has a scorecard too.

Most people avoid it for the same reason golfers sometimes do. It can feel confronting. It can feel disappointing. It can expose mistakes you would rather forget. But just like golf, avoiding the scorecard does not protect you. It removes awareness, and without awareness, every decision gets harder.

Reading your financial scorecard is not about judgment. It is about clarity. It is about knowing where you stand so you can play the rest of the round intelligently.

Income, expenses, and cash flow

In golf, you know your yardages. Or at least you should.

Knowing how far you hit each club determines every shot you take. If you guess, you misclub. If you misclub, you short-side yourself or bring hazards into play. Financially, income and expenses are your distances.

Income is how much money comes in. Salary, bonuses, prize money, stipends, NIL income, side work. Expenses are how much goes out. Rent, food, travel, subscriptions, insurance, lifestyle choices. Cash flow is the space between those two numbers.

That space determines everything.

Positive cash flow means you have margin. Margin creates options. It allows you to save, invest, absorb surprises, and make decisions without panic. Negative cash flow forces reactions. It pushes people toward debt, desperation, and bad choices.

Many athletes know their income but underestimate their expenses. Small purchases feel harmless in isolation. Just like missed fairways or lip-out putts, they do not feel like a big deal in the moment. Over time, they stack up.

Golfers understand this pattern. One poor decision rarely ruins a round. A series of careless decisions almost always does. Cash flow works the same way. Leaks matter more than people realize.

Understanding cash flow is not about cutting joy out of life. It is about knowing the terrain you are playing on. You cannot choose smart shots if you do not know your distances.

Assets, liabilities, and net worth

Golfers track penalties because penalties change the round.

Assets and liabilities are the financial version of that concept. Assets are things that help you move forward. Savings accounts, investment accounts, retirement plans, and property that builds value over time. Liabilities are obligations that slow you down. Loans, credit card balances, and ongoing financial commitments.

Net worth is simply the difference between the two.

Many people fixate on income and ignore net worth. That is like focusing only on how far you hit the ball without caring where it lands. High income paired with high debt still creates pressure. Modest income paired with low obligations can create stability.

Net worth is not a scoreboard to compare yourself to others. It is more like a handicap. It gives context. It tells you where you are starting from so improvement makes sense.

Golfers who ignore their handicap often set unrealistic expectations. Financially, people do the same thing when they do not understand their net worth. They expect outcomes that do not match their starting position, then get frustrated when progress feels slow.

Clarity fixes that.

Fixed vs variable expenses

Not all expenses behave the same way.

Fixed expenses are predictable. Rent or mortgage payments. Insurance premiums. Loan payments. These are like tee shots on holes you have played many times. You know the distance. You know the danger. There is not much flexibility.

Variable expenses change based on behavior. Food. Travel. Entertainment. Shopping. These are approach shots affected by wind, lie, and decision-making. This is where most control exists.

Many people try to cut fixed expenses first because they feel large and obvious. Often, that is not realistic. Variable expenses are where discipline actually shows up. Golfers understand this instinctively. You cannot change the length of the hole, but you can choose where to aim and how aggressive to be.

Understanding which expenses are fixed and which are flexible gives you leverage. It turns money from something that happens to you into something you manage.

Tracking where your money actually goes

Most golfers think they know where their shots go until they look at shot data or film.

Money is no different.

People are often surprised when they review bank statements or credit card activity. Patterns appear that were invisible in the moment. Subscriptions forgotten. Small purchases repeated. Lifestyle creep disguised as normal behavior.

Tracking is not punishment. It is feedback.

Golfers rely on feedback constantly. Launch monitors. Yardage books. Scorecards. Film. None of those tools exist to shame players. They exist to make improvement possible.

Tracking money is financial film study.

You do not need perfection. You need consistency. A simple system reviewed regularly beats an elaborate system you abandon. Golfers know this lesson well. Reps matter more than gear.

Game situations and decision points

Imagine this scenario.

You are six holes into a round and you realize you are three over par. The swing feels fine, but the scorecard says otherwise. Do you start forcing shots to get it back immediately, or do you tighten up, trust your game plan, and let the round unfold?

Financially, this happens when expenses run higher than expected. The wrong move is panic or avoidance. The right move is awareness and adjustment.

Another scenario.

You check your scorecard at the turn and you are under par. Confidence is high. Do you suddenly start firing at every pin, or do you respect the course and protect your position?

Income increases create the same temptation. Without a scorecard mindset, confidence turns into overextension.

The scorecard guides decisions. It does not dictate emotion.

Common athlete mistakes and financial parallels

One common athlete mistake is avoiding numbers because they feel negative. Golfers who refuse to add up the score mid-round often spiral because they lose strategy. Financially, avoiding statements and balances creates the same loss of control.

Another mistake is focusing only on offense. Athletes want to score. Financially, that means earning and investing while ignoring expenses and liabilities. Great golfers play defense too. Avoiding big numbers matters.

A third mistake is comparison. Golfers who obsess over someone else's score forget their own plan. Financially, comparison drives reckless decisions. Your scorecard is your responsibility.

Winning the long game

Reading the scorecard does not guarantee a great round. It gives you a chance to play smart.

Once you understand your income, expenses, assets, liabilities, and habits, money becomes calmer. Decisions feel grounded. Emotion loses power. You stop guessing and start managing.

Golfers who respect the scorecard do not fear it. They use it. Your financial snapshot deserves the same respect.

Athlete Takeaways

- The scorecard tells the truth whether you look at it or not
- Cash flow is your margin for error and opportunity
- Net worth gives context, not judgment
- Variable expenses are where discipline wins rounds
- Tracking money is film study that leads to improvement

Chapter 3: Eliminating Penalty Strokes: Budgeting and Saving

Penalty strokes ruin good rounds.

You can hit great shots all day and still walk off the course frustrated because of a few avoidable mistakes. A ball out of bounds. A hazard you did not respect. A risky decision when a simple play would have kept you in position. Great golfers are not perfect. They are disciplined about avoiding damage.

Budgeting and saving exist for the same reason.

They are not about restriction. They are about protection. They keep small mistakes from turning into big numbers that derail the entire round.

Most people dislike budgeting because they misunderstand what it is. They picture spreadsheets, deprivation, and constant self-denial. Golfers used to think course management was boring too. Then they realized it was how tournaments are actually won.

Budgeting systems that actually work

In golf, the best strategy is the one you will actually follow.

A complicated game plan that falls apart under pressure is useless. The same is true with budgeting. The best budgeting system is not the most detailed one. It is the one that fits your life and gets used consistently.

Budgeting is simply deciding where your money goes before it disappears.

At its core, a budget answers three questions. How much comes in. How much goes out. Where the difference should go. That is it. Everything else is preference.

Some people like detailed line items. Others prefer broad categories. Some use apps. Others use spreadsheets or simple rules. There is no single right system. What matters is clarity and repetition.

Golfers understand this instinctively. Some players are feel-based. Others are technical. Both can succeed if they commit to their approach. Financial discipline works the same way.

A common athlete mistake is assuming budgeting means cutting everything fun. In reality, budgeting creates permission. When you know what is set aside for savings and obligations, you can enjoy the rest without guilt. That confidence reduces stress and impulsive decisions.

Automating savings like practice reps

Great golfers do not rely on motivation. They rely on routine.

They practice even when they are tired. They show up even when they do not feel sharp. Progress comes from reps, not inspiration. Saving money works the same way.

Automation is financial repetition.

When savings happen automatically, they do not depend on willpower. Money moves before you have a chance to spend it. This mirrors how athletes build habits through structured practice schedules.

Automated savings turn good intentions into action. Direct transfers to savings accounts. Automatic contributions to retirement accounts. Scheduled investment deposits. These systems remove emotion from the decision.

Many athletes wait to save what is left over. That is like practicing only if there is time after everything else. It rarely happens. Smart golfers schedule practice first. Smart savers do the same.

Automation also smooths inconsistency. Income may fluctuate. Motivation may fade. Automated systems keep progress moving quietly in the background.

Emergency funds as financial protection

Emergency funds are boring.

They do not grow fast. They do not feel impressive. They rarely get talked about. Yet they are one of the most important parts of financial stability.

In golf terms, an emergency fund is your recovery shot.

It keeps one bad break from turning into a disaster. A medical bill. A car repair. A travel issue. A temporary income disruption. Without an emergency fund, these events force penalty strokes like credit card debt or early withdrawals from long-term investments.

Great golfers respect trouble areas. They know where hazards are and plan accordingly. Emergency savings do the same thing. They acknowledge reality instead of pretending life will be smooth.

An emergency fund creates emotional stability too. Knowing you can handle surprises reduces anxiety and prevents rushed decisions. That calm matters.

Many athletes resist emergency savings because it feels like money sitting idle. Golfers once resisted laying up because it felt passive. Experience teaches otherwise. Staying in position matters more than occasional hero shots.

Balancing lifestyle with long-term goals

This is where budgeting often breaks down.

Athletes work hard. They train relentlessly. They sacrifice time and energy. Wanting to enjoy life is reasonable. The problem arises when lifestyle choices ignore long-term consequences.

Golfers manage this balance constantly. You want to attack when the opportunity is right. You also need to protect against risk. Every hole requires judgment.

Financially, balance means aligning spending with values and goals. It does not mean saying no to everything. It means saying yes intentionally.

One common mistake is lifestyle creep. Income increases and spending quietly follows. Golfers see this too. Confidence leads to unnecessary aggression. Over time, mistakes accumulate.

Budgeting helps define boundaries. It clarifies what matters most. Travel. Experiences. Hobbies. Security. Giving. Once priorities are clear, trade-offs become easier.

This balance is not static. It changes with seasons of life. Early career. Peak earning years. Transitions. Adjustments are normal. The system should flex without breaking.

Game situations and decision points

Picture this.

You are standing on a hole with water guarding the green. You can reach it with a perfect shot. The smarter play is laying up to a comfortable distance. What do you do?

Financially, this mirrors choosing between spending now and saving for later. The aggressive option may feel exciting. The disciplined option keeps you in control.

Another scenario.

You just had a great stretch of holes. Confidence is high. Do you abandon your game plan, or do you stay disciplined?

Income bonuses and windfalls create the same test. Without a plan, extra money disappears quickly. With a plan, it accelerates progress.

Common athlete mistakes and financial parallels

One mistake is relying on discipline instead of systems. Athletes know discipline fades under fatigue. Systems exist to protect against that. Budgeting and automation are systems.

Another mistake is avoiding planning because it feels restrictive. Golfers who refuse strategy often make harder shots than necessary. Structure creates freedom.

A third mistake is reacting emotionally to setbacks. One unexpected expense does not mean the plan failed. It means the plan worked by absorbing the hit.

Winning the long game

Great rounds are not defined by highlight shots. They are defined by avoided disasters.

Budgeting and saving eliminate penalty strokes. They create stability. They protect momentum. They allow long-term strategies to work.

You do not need perfection. You need consistency.

When budgeting becomes routine and saving becomes automatic, money stops feeling chaotic. It becomes manageable. Predictable. Boring in the best way.

That is how championships are won.

Athlete Takeaways

- Penalty strokes hurt more than missed birdie chances
- The best budget is the one you actually follow
- Automate savings the same way you schedule practice
- Emergency funds keep one bad break from ruining the round
- Discipline plus systems beats motivation every time

Chapter 4: Credit, Debt, and Hazard Shots

Every golfer knows where the trouble is before they ever swing. Water down the left. Bunkers guarding the green. Out of bounds creeping closer the farther you try to hit it. Hazard shots are not surprises. They are printed on the course map. The problem is not that hazards exist. The problem is pretending they do not matter.

Credit and debt are financial hazards.

They are not automatically bad. They are not automatically good. Like hazards on a course, they require respect, planning, and smart decision-making. Golfers who ignore trouble areas eventually pay for it. Financially, people who misunderstand credit and debt often see their scorecard blow up slowly, then suddenly.

This chapter is about learning how to see hazards clearly, understand the rules, and decide when to play near them and when to stay far away.

How credit scores and reports work

Think of your credit score like your reputation on tour.

It is not about one swing. It is built over time based on behavior. How often you show up. How responsibly you play. How you handle mistakes. A single bad hole rarely defines a career, but repeated poor decisions do.

A credit score is a numerical summary of your borrowing behavior. It reflects whether you pay bills on time, how much debt you carry, how long you have used credit, and how often you apply for new credit. Lenders use it to decide whether they will let you play on their course and what conditions they will impose.

Your credit report is the detailed scorecard.

It lists accounts, balances, payment history, and any negative marks. Just like a golf scorecard, it does not care how you feel about the round. It records what happened.

Many athletes never check their credit report until something goes wrong. That is like waiting until the final hole to add up the score. Reviewing it regularly helps catch errors, understand patterns, and make adjustments before damage compounds.

Credit scores are not moral judgments. They are tools. Used correctly, they provide access. Used poorly, they create obstacles.

Credit cards, loans, and interest

Credit cards and loans are clubs in the bag.

Used correctly, they serve a purpose. Used carelessly, they cause damage.

A credit card allows you to borrow short-term money. If you pay it off quickly, the cost is minimal. If you carry balances, interest starts compounding against you. That compounding works the opposite direction of investing. Instead of helping you, it works relentlessly to increase what you owe.

Interest is the hazard.

Many people focus on minimum payments without understanding what interest is doing behind the scenes. That is like knowing where the fairway is but ignoring the slope toward trouble. The shot may look fine initially, but gravity takes over.

Loans work similarly but over longer time frames. Student loans, auto loans, personal loans, mortgages. Each has different rules, rates, and purposes. The danger is not borrowing itself. The danger is borrowing without understanding cost, duration, and impact on flexibility.

Golfers study yardages before selecting clubs. Borrowers need to understand interest rates, terms, and total cost before taking on debt.

Good debt vs bad debt

This is one of the most misunderstood concepts in personal finance.

Good debt does not mean safe. Bad debt does not mean evil. These labels describe how debt is used and what it produces.

Good debt generally supports long-term goals, income growth, or asset building. Examples include education that increases earning potential or a reasonable mortgage for housing stability. Even then, good debt still carries risk and requires discipline.

Bad debt usually funds consumption without long-term benefit. High-interest credit cards used for lifestyle spending. Loans taken to support habits rather than progress. These debts often provide short-term pleasure and long-term pressure.

In golf terms, good debt is playing aggressively when the conditions are right and the upside is worth the risk. Bad debt is forcing shots that bring hazards into play with little reward.

The key is intention and restraint. Debt should serve a purpose you understand, not impulses you regret later.

Debt mistakes that destroy scorecards

Some debt mistakes are common enough to be predictable.

One mistake is using credit to cover lifestyle gaps instead of fixing cash flow. That is like playing from the rough every hole and pretending the lie will improve on its own. Debt masks problems temporarily while making them worse long-term.

Another mistake is carrying balances because minimum payments feel manageable. Minimum payments are deceptive. They make the round feel under control while the score quietly climbs.

A third mistake is taking on debt without understanding terms. Adjustable rates. Deferred interest. Fees buried in fine print. Golfers would never play a course without knowing where hazards are. Financially, people do this all the time.

Another common error is emotional borrowing. Stress, comparison, and pressure push people to spend beyond their plan. Golfers force shots when frustrated. Borrowers do the same.

Game situations and decision points

Imagine standing on a hole with water down the entire left side.

You can aim safely right and accept a longer approach, or you can challenge the water to shorten the hole. The choice depends on conditions, confidence, and the scorecard.

Financially, this mirrors using credit strategically versus recklessly. A planned purchase with a payoff strategy is different from reacting emotionally.

Another scenario.

You are already in trouble. The ball is in the trees. Do you attempt a miracle shot that could make things worse, or do you punch out and recover?

Debt recovery works the same way. Aggressive fixes often fail. Simple, disciplined steps usually work better.

Common athlete mistakes and financial parallels

Athletes are used to pushing limits. That mindset can create problems with credit. Borrowing feels like leverage until it becomes a burden.

Another mistake is trusting confidence over understanding. Credit card offers sound easy. Golfers know easy swings still require good setup.

A final mistake is ignoring the scoreboard. Avoiding balances, statements, and interest calculations allows problems to grow quietly.

Winning the long game

Credit and debt are not enemies. They are hazards.

Great golfers respect hazards. They plan around them. They understand the rules and consequences. Financial success requires the same mindset.

Used wisely, credit supports progress. Used carelessly, it destroys scorecards.

The goal is not fear. The goal is control.

Athlete Takeaways

- Hazards are only dangerous when you ignore them
- Credit scores reflect habits, not talent
- Interest compounds against you if you let it
- Good debt has purpose, bad debt has excuses
- Recovery shots beat miracle swings every time

Chapter 5: The Golf Bag of Money: Banking Basics

Every golfer knows what happens when the bag is wrong.

Too many clubs you never use. Missing the one club you actually need. No idea where anything is when the moment matters. The round feels harder than it should because the setup is sloppy. Great golfers do not obsess over gear, but they are intentional about what is in the bag and how it is used.

Your banking system is your golf bag for money.

It is not flashy. It does not win tournaments by itself. But if it is poorly organized, every financial decision becomes more difficult. When your accounts are set up correctly, money moves smoothly, mistakes are easier to avoid, and discipline becomes automatic.

This chapter is about understanding the basic clubs in the bag and how to use them correctly.

Checking vs savings accounts

Checking and savings accounts serve different purposes, just like different clubs.

A checking account is your everyday club. It is where income lands and bills get paid. It is designed for movement. Frequent transactions. Convenience. Accessibility. This is the club you use most often.

A savings account is a position club. It is not meant for constant action. It exists to create separation between money you plan to spend and money you plan to protect. Emergency funds, short-term goals, and planned expenses belong here.

Many people blur these roles, and that creates problems.

Keeping too much money in checking makes it easy to overspend. Keeping everything in savings creates friction and confusion. Golfers understand this instinctively. You do not use a driver for every shot, and you do not use a putter from the fairway.

Separation creates discipline.

When money has a clear job, behavior improves. Bills get paid from checking. Savings stays intact unless there is a real reason to use it. This structure reduces emotional decisions.

Savings accounts also provide psychological safety. Knowing there is money set aside for unexpected events changes how you approach decisions. Confidence increases. Panic decreases.

Online banks vs traditional banks

Choosing a bank is like choosing where to practice.

Some golfers prefer a local course they know well. Others like range access anywhere they travel. Both can work. The key is understanding the differences.

Traditional banks often offer physical branches. That can be helpful for in-person service, cash handling, or complex issues. They may bundle services like loans or business accounts. The tradeoff is often lower interest on savings and higher fees.

Online banks usually offer higher interest on savings and fewer fees. Their systems are built for efficiency. The tradeoff is less in-person interaction.

Neither option is inherently better.

The right choice depends on how you use money. If you value convenience and high savings rates, online banks often work well. If you need branch access or prefer face-to-face service, traditional banks may fit better.

Many people use a combination. Checking at a traditional bank. Savings at an online bank. This mirrors how golfers use different facilities for different purposes.

The mistake is not the choice. The mistake is staying in a setup that does not serve you because it feels familiar.

How money moves electronically

Understanding how money moves is like understanding ball flight.

You do not need to be an engineer, but you should know what happens when you swing. Financially, electronic movement includes direct deposit, transfers, bill pay, and card transactions.

Direct deposit is income automation. Money moves without effort. This is ideal. It removes delay and reduces temptation.

Transfers move money between accounts. Scheduled transfers support savings goals. Manual transfers require discipline. Golfers know routine beats intention.

Electronic bill pay reduces missed payments. Missed payments hurt credit and create stress. Automation protects against that.

Debit cards provide immediate access to checking funds. Credit cards provide delayed payment but carry risk if balances grow. Understanding timing matters. Spending money you already have is different from spending borrowed money.

Money moves fast now. That speed increases convenience and risk. Awareness keeps speed from becoming a problem.

Fraud protection and overdraft control

Fraud is the financial equivalent of an unexpected hazard.

It can happen even when you do things right. That is why protection matters.

Banks offer tools to reduce risk. Alerts for transactions. Limits on transfers. The ability to freeze cards quickly. These features are not optional. They are defensive strategy.

Monitoring accounts regularly helps catch issues early. Golfers check lies and conditions before swinging. Financial awareness works the same way.

Overdrafts are another common problem.

An overdraft happens when spending exceeds available funds. Fees pile up quickly. It is like stepping into a bunker repeatedly because you are not paying attention.

Some banks allow overdraft protection through linked savings accounts. Others allow transactions to be declined. Declining a transaction may feel embarrassing, but it is far less damaging than repeated fees.

Control matters more than convenience.

Game situations and decision points

Imagine this scenario.

You are on a course with tight fairways. Do you keep swinging driver because it feels powerful, or do you choose a club that keeps you in play?

Financially, this mirrors choosing convenience over structure. Swiping without awareness feels easy until it causes problems.

Another scenario.

You keep emergency money in your checking account because it is accessible. Over time, it disappears. A better setup would have protected it.

The bag matters.

Common athlete mistakes and financial parallels

One mistake is using one account for everything. Golfers who try to play an entire round with one club struggle.

Another mistake is ignoring fees. Small fees feel harmless. Over time, they add strokes.

A third mistake is assuming banking is boring and unimportant. Golfers know equipment setup matters even if it is not exciting.

Winning the long game

Banking basics are not about maximizing returns. They are about minimizing mistakes.

When the bag is organized, decisions feel easier. Discipline improves. Stress decreases. Everything else in your financial game benefits.

You do not need a perfect system. You need a functional one.

Set up the bag correctly, and the rest of the round becomes manageable.

Athlete Takeaways

- The right bag makes every shot easier
- Checking is for movement, savings is for protection
- Separation creates discipline without effort
- Automation beats motivation every time
- Control and awareness prevent avoidable penalty strokes

Part II: Course Management, Defense, and Protection

Great rounds are built by avoiding big mistakes.

Great golf is rarely about how many spectacular shots you hit. It is about how few disasters you allow.

Watch elite players over four rounds and a pattern emerges. They respect the course. They know where the danger is. They understand that one reckless decision can undo hours of good work. Birdies help, but doubles and triples destroy momentum. Championships are won by players who manage risk, protect position, and stay disciplined when conditions turn against them.

Money works the same way.

Most long-term financial damage does not come from lack of opportunity. It comes from avoidable mistakes. Poor risk awareness. Inadequate protection. Overconfidence. Ignoring downside. People often focus on how to make more money without thinking enough about how to keep what they already have.

This part of the book is about defense.

In sports, defense does not mean playing scared. It means playing smart. It means understanding that staying in position gives you more chances to win. Financial defense works the same way. When you protect against obvious risks, you give your long-term plans room to work.

Course management in golf starts with awareness. You study the layout. You know where trouble lives. You plan your shots accordingly. Financial course management requires the same mindset. You need to understand risk before you encounter it. You need to think through consequences before decisions are forced on you.

Many athletes struggle here because risk feels abstract until it shows up. In sports, consequences are immediate. A bad shot is visible. Financial consequences often arrive later. An uncovered risk can sit quietly for years before causing damage. That delay makes it easy to ignore protection until it is too late.

Defense also requires humility.

Great golfers accept that they are not immune to bad breaks. Weather changes. Lies vary. Bodies get tired. They prepare for this reality instead of pretending it will not happen. Financial planning demands the same honesty. Illness, accidents, lawsuits, income disruption, and market volatility are not signs of failure. They are part of life.

This section focuses on understanding risk, choosing smart shots, and building protection into your financial game. Insurance, liability coverage, and income protection are not exciting topics. They do not feel like offense. But they are what allow offense to work without constant fear.

In golf, players often talk about playing within themselves. That does not mean playing small. It means knowing your tendencies and respecting them. Financially, playing within yourself means matching risk to reality. Income stability. Time horizon. Family responsibilities. Emotional tolerance. These factors matter more than hypothetical returns.

Another key concept in this section is control.

Golfers control what they can. Setup. Alignment. Club selection. Commitment. They cannot control bounces or weather. Financially, control looks like having the right coverage, clear beneficiaries, and systems that reduce exposure to catastrophic loss. You cannot control markets or life events, but you can control preparation.

Many people view insurance and protection as wasted money because nothing happens most of the time. Golfers once viewed laying up the same way. Experience teaches otherwise. The value is not in the frequency of use. It is in the avoidance of disaster.

This part of the book also reinforces the idea that defense supports confidence. When you know hazards are accounted for, you swing more freely. When you know your financial base is protected, decisions feel calmer. Emotion loses power. Pressure becomes manageable.

Part II is not about fear. It is about respect.

Respect for risk. Respect for uncertainty. Respect for the fact that long-term success requires staying in the game. Great rounds are not built by forcing shots into danger. They are built by making smart decisions, avoiding big mistakes, and giving yourself chances hole after hole.

The chapters that follow will help you see financial hazards clearly, choose smarter shots, and build protection that allows the rest of your plan to work as intended. When defense is solid, offense becomes easier.

That is true on the course. It is true with money.

Chapter 6: Risk Awareness and Shot Selection

Every golfer learns this lesson the hard way.

There are shots you *can* hit and shots you *should* hit. On the range, with no pressure, many shots feel possible. On the course, with hazards, wind, and a scorecard that matters, the smart choice often looks different. The best golfers are not the ones who attempt the hardest shots. They are the ones who choose the right shot for the situation.

Risk awareness is what separates skill from judgment.

Money decisions work the same way. Many people get into trouble not because they lack options, but because they misunderstand risk. They confuse confidence with control. They confuse possibility with probability. They swing when they should lay up.

This chapter is about learning how to see risk clearly and choose shots that support long-term success.

Emotional vs financial risk

In golf, emotional risk and physical risk are different things.

Standing over a shot with water left and out of bounds right creates emotional pressure. The heart rate rises. Doubt creeps in. That emotional response can cause a poor swing even if the shot itself is reasonable.

Financially, emotional risk works the same way. Market swings, social comparison, headlines, and fear trigger reactions that feel urgent but are not always rational. Many bad money decisions are emotional responses to discomfort rather than thoughtful evaluations of risk.

Financial risk, on the other hand, is the actual potential for loss.

A shot over water carries a known downside. A highly concentrated investment carries a known downside. Emotional risk is how it *feels*. Financial risk is what can *actually happen*. Confusing the two leads to mistakes.

Golfers learn to slow down and separate emotion from execution. Financial discipline requires the same pause.

Time horizon and flexibility

Every shot in golf depends on context.

A par five on the first hole plays differently than a par five on the eighteenth with a lead. Time matters. Position matters. Flexibility matters.

Financial decisions are inseparable from time horizon.

Money needed next month should not be exposed to the same risk as money needed in twenty years. Short-term goals require stability. Long-term goals allow volatility. Mixing these horizons is one of the most common financial errors.

Flexibility matters too. Golfers with multiple shot options adapt better to conditions. Financial flexibility comes from savings, low fixed expenses, and manageable obligations. The more flexible you are, the more risk you can absorb without panic.

Without flexibility, even small risks feel overwhelming.

How risk affects every money decision

Risk is not limited to investing.

It shows up in spending, saving, borrowing, career choices, and lifestyle decisions. Choosing a high fixed-cost lifestyle increases risk. Carrying high-interest debt increases risk. Ignoring insurance increases risk.

Golfers think in terms of risk constantly. Where is the miss? What happens if this goes wrong? Financial decisions deserve the same thought process.

Ignoring risk does not eliminate it. It concentrates it.

Knowing when to attack and when to lay up

This is the heart of smart golf.

Attacking when the conditions are right creates opportunity. Laying up when risk outweighs reward preserves position. The key is knowing the difference.

Financially, attacking might mean investing aggressively for long-term growth when income is stable and time horizon is long. Laying up might mean prioritizing savings, debt reduction, or protection when uncertainty is high.

Neither approach is permanent. Both require adjustment as circumstances change.

Game situations and decision points

You are two strokes back with three holes to play. The pin is tucked behind a bunker. Do you fire at it or aim center green?

Financially, this mirrors chasing high returns versus protecting progress. The decision depends on position, not ego.

Another scenario.

You are early in the round with plenty of holes left. Forcing shots early rarely helps. The same is true financially. Early mistakes compound over time.

Common athlete mistakes and financial parallels

One mistake is overestimating control. Golfers know even great swings do not guarantee outcomes. Financial markets work the same way.

Another mistake is letting emotion dictate strategy. Frustration leads to forced shots. Fear leads to abandoning plans. Awareness reduces both.

A third mistake is copying others. Just because someone else attacked successfully does not mean the shot was right for you.

Winning the long game

Risk awareness is not about fear. It is about clarity.

Great golfers respect risk and make decisions that keep them in position. Financial success demands the same discipline.

Choosing the right shot matters more than swinging hard.

Athlete Takeaways

- Not every shot you can hit is a shot you should take
- Separate how risk feels from what risk actually is
- Match risk to time horizon and flexibility
- Attack with intention, lay up with confidence
- Smart decisions keep you in the tournament

Chapter 7: Insurance Fundamentals Every Player Needs

Every golfer knows this truth, even if they do not like it.

You cannot control bad breaks.

You can hit a perfect shot and get a terrible bounce. Weather changes. Lies are uneven. Sometimes the course wins. Great golfers do not pretend these things will not happen. They plan for them. They respect the reality of risk and build protection into their strategy so one bad break does not ruin the entire round.

Insurance exists for the same reason.

It is not exciting. It does not feel like progress. It does not help you score birdies. But it keeps one unexpected event from wiping out years of disciplined work. Insurance is financial defense. And just like defense in sports, it only gets appreciated after it does its job.

This chapter is about understanding the insurance coverage every player needs and why skipping protection is one of the most expensive mistakes athletes make.

Health insurance basics

Health insurance is the most important coverage most people will ever have.

Your body is your engine. For athletes especially, physical health affects everything. Training, earning ability, confidence, and quality of life all depend on it. Ignoring health insurance is like walking onto the course without shoes and hoping for the best.

Health insurance helps cover the cost of medical care, from routine visits to serious emergencies. Without it, even a minor issue can turn into a financial disaster.

Key concepts matter here.

Premiums are what you pay to keep coverage active. Deductibles are what you pay out of pocket before insurance starts covering costs. Copays and coinsurance are how costs are shared after that point. Coverage networks determine which doctors and facilities are included.

Many athletes choose plans based only on the monthly premium. That is a mistake. A low premium paired with a very high deductible may leave you exposed if something happens. On the other hand, the most expensive plan may not be necessary if you rarely use medical services.

This is about balance.

Golfers choose clubs based on conditions. Health insurance should be chosen based on your health, lifestyle, and financial flexibility. The goal is not to guess. The goal is to understand trade-offs and avoid catastrophic exposure.

Auto and renters insurance

Auto insurance is mandatory for a reason.

Cars are expensive. Accidents happen quickly. Liability can be massive. Auto insurance protects you from financial ruin when something goes wrong on the road.

At a minimum, liability coverage is essential. It protects you if you injure someone or damage their property. Medical payments coverage helps with injuries. Collision and comprehensive coverage protect your vehicle.

Many athletes focus only on insuring the car. They ignore liability limits. That is dangerous.

In golf terms, this is like worrying about the ball and ignoring where it might land. Liability claims follow you, not the car. Higher limits are often inexpensive relative to the protection they provide.

Renters insurance is one of the most overlooked policies.

If you rent, your landlord's insurance does not cover your belongings. Renters insurance protects personal property and provides liability coverage. It also covers temporary living expenses if your place becomes uninhabitable.

Renters insurance is usually inexpensive. Skipping it to save a small amount of money exposes you to large risk. That trade-off does not make sense.

Homeowners insurance

Homeowners insurance protects one of the largest financial commitments most people ever make.

It covers the structure, personal belongings, liability, and additional living expenses if the home is damaged. Fires, storms, theft, and accidents happen even when you are careful.

One of the biggest mistakes homeowners make is underinsuring their property. Coverage should reflect replacement cost, not market value. The cost to rebuild may be very different from what you paid for the home.

Deductibles matter here as well. A higher deductible lowers premiums but increases out-of-pocket exposure. This only works if you have the cash to cover it. Otherwise, the plan fails when you need it most.

Golfers understand preparation for worst-case scenarios. Homeowners insurance is no different. It is not about expecting disaster. It is about being ready if it happens.

Deductibles, premiums, and coverage limits

These are the levers of insurance.

Premiums are the cost of entry. Deductibles are your share of the risk. Coverage limits define how much protection you actually have.

Many people focus only on premium cost. That is like choosing a course based only on green fees and ignoring difficulty. Cheap coverage that does not protect you is not a bargain.

Coverage limits are critical. Liability limits should reflect what you could lose, not what feels comfortable. Athletes with future earning potential should be especially careful here. Protecting future income is just as important as protecting current assets.

Insurance is about transferring risk you cannot afford to keep.

Small risks can be self-insured. Big risks should not be. Knowing the difference is part of financial maturity.

Game situations and decision points

Imagine you are playing a course with deep bunkers and water hazards. You can ignore them and hope for the best, or you can plan your shots to minimize exposure.

Insurance decisions work the same way.

Do you choose minimum coverage because it is cheaper, or do you choose adequate coverage because you understand downside risk?

Another scenario.

You increase your income and responsibilities but never update coverage. That is like playing a longer course with the same clubs and strategy. Adjustments matter.

Common athlete mistakes and financial parallels

One common mistake is assuming nothing will happen. Golfers know better. Bad breaks are part of the game.

Another mistake is viewing insurance as wasted money. It feels that way until the moment it saves you.

A third mistake is buying coverage without understanding it. Policies should be reviewed periodically. Life changes require updates.

Winning the long game

Insurance does not help you score. It helps you stay in the game.

Great golfers protect against disaster so their skill and discipline can shine over time. Financially, insurance does the same thing. It protects progress. It preserves options. It keeps one bad moment from undoing years of work.

Defense is not weakness. It is intelligence.

Athlete Takeaways

- Defense keeps one bad break from ending the round
- Health insurance protects your most valuable asset
- Liability coverage matters more than you think
- Cheap coverage that fails is not a bargain
- Protect the long game so offense can work

Chapter 8: Life, Disability, and Liability Protection

Every golfer knows there are risks you cannot see on the scorecard. A sudden storm. A slip on wet grass. A freak bounce that sends the ball somewhere you never planned. These moments are rare, but when they happen, they matter. The best players do not pretend they are immune. They plan for the unexpected so one bad break does not end the round.

Life, disability, and liability protection exist for the same reason.

They protect against risks that are low frequency but high impact. These are not everyday inconveniences. These are events that can permanently alter your financial trajectory if you are unprepared. This chapter is about protecting income, protecting people who depend on you, and protecting yourself from lawsuits and claims that can follow you for years.

Term vs permanent life insurance

Life insurance answers a simple question.

If you are not here tomorrow, who is financially affected and how badly?

Life insurance is not about you. It is about the people who depend on your income, support, or presence. Family. Partners. Children. Even business partners in some cases.

Term life insurance is straightforward.

You choose a coverage amount and a time period. If you pass away during that period, the benefit pays out. If not, the policy expires. Term insurance is typically inexpensive and efficient. It covers the years when financial risk is highest, like raising children, paying down debt, or building a career.

Permanent life insurance lasts for your entire life and includes a savings component. It is more complex and more expensive. It can make sense in specific situations, such as estate planning or charitable strategies, but it is not a default choice.

Many athletes are sold permanent insurance too early because it sounds sophisticated. Golfers know that advanced clubs do not fix poor fundamentals. The same logic applies here. For most people, term insurance covers the real risk at a reasonable cost.

The right amount of coverage depends on income, obligations, and future goals. Guessing is not a strategy. Clarity matters.

Disability insurance and income protection

Disability insurance is often more important than life insurance.

Why?

Because the risk of being injured or ill and unable to work is far higher than the risk of dying during your working years. For athletes, this reality is especially clear. Bodies break down. Injuries happen. Careers change unexpectedly.

Disability insurance protects your income if you cannot work due to illness or injury. It replaces a portion of earnings so bills still get paid and goals remain intact.

Many people assume disability coverage is unnecessary or covered by their employer. Often, employer coverage is limited, short-term, or tied to employment status. For athletes, self-employed individuals, or those with variable income, personal coverage is critical.

The most important feature is definition of disability. Strong policies protect your ability to do your specific job, not just any job. This distinction matters.

In golf terms, this is the difference between being allowed to play your usual course or being forced onto a course that does not match your skills. Protecting your specific income stream matters.

Disability insurance keeps one injury from becoming a permanent financial setback.

Umbrella liability coverage

Umbrella insurance protects against lawsuits and liability claims that exceed basic policy limits.

Auto and homeowners insurance provide some liability coverage, but limits may be lower than you think. If a serious accident occurs, those limits can be exhausted quickly. Anything beyond that comes out of your pocket.

Umbrella coverage adds an extra layer of protection. It covers large claims and legal costs across multiple situations. It is often surprisingly affordable relative to the protection it provides.

Athletes with public visibility, assets, or future earning potential face elevated liability risk. One incident can create long-term consequences.

In golf terms, umbrella insurance is like knowing there is space beyond the fairway. It gives margin. It allows you to play confidently without constantly fearing disaster.

Common insurance mistakes athletes make

One common mistake is assuming youth equals safety. Athletes feel strong. Healthy. Invincible. That mindset ignores probability and consequences. Golfers learn quickly that confidence does not eliminate hazards.

Another mistake is underinsuring to save money. Minimum coverage feels cheaper until it fails. Insurance should be sized to risk, not comfort.

A third mistake is failing to update coverage as life changes. Income increases. Families grow. Assets accumulate. Coverage that made sense years ago may be insufficient now.

Another mistake is confusing insurance with investing. Insurance transfers risk. Investing builds wealth. Mixing those goals creates confusion and inefficiency.

Finally, many athletes avoid reviewing policies because the language feels overwhelming. Avoidance is not protection. Understanding matters.

Game situations and decision points

Imagine standing on a hole with water long and out of bounds short.

You can swing freely and hope, or you can choose a shot that respects the danger. Insurance decisions work the same way. You decide how much risk you are willing to keep and how much you transfer.

Another scenario.

Your swing speed increases, but you never adjust club selection. Coverage should evolve as income and responsibilities change.

Winning the long game

Life, disability, and liability protection are not about pessimism. They are about respect for reality.

Great golfers prepare for bad breaks so they can focus on execution. Financial protection does the same thing. It removes fear from decision-making and allows progress to continue even when life gets unpredictable.

Defense is not passive. It is proactive.

Protect the income you depend on. Protect the people who depend on you. Protect yourself from risks that can derail everything else.

That is how long careers and stable financial lives are built.

Athlete Takeaways

- Protect people and income before chasing upside
- Term insurance covers risk efficiently for most players
- Disability risk is higher than most people admit
- Umbrella coverage adds margin when stakes are high
- Updating protection is part of staying in the game

Part III: Constructing the Shot (Investing Fundamentals)

High-percentage shots beat heroic swings.

Every golfer loves the idea of the perfect shot.

The towering draw that lands softly. The long iron that carries the trouble and stops near the pin. The highlight moment that looks effortless and feels unforgettable. Those shots exist, but they are not how great rounds are built. Great rounds are built by choosing shots you can repeat, not shots you can describe afterward.

Investing works the same way.

Most people approach investing the way amateurs approach golf. They chase distance. They look for something impressive. They copy what worked for someone else without understanding why. They swing hard, hope for the best, and are surprised when inconsistency shows up.

This part of the book is about constructing the shot properly.

In golf, shot construction starts before the swing. You assess the lie. You read the wind. You choose the club. You visualize the shot shape. Then you commit. Investing requires the same discipline. Markets move. Conditions change. But the process remains constant.

High-percentage shots are repeatable.

They may not make highlights, but they keep you in position. They reduce mistakes. They give you more chances to succeed over time. In investing, this means understanding how markets actually work, respecting risk, diversifying intelligently, and staying patient when things feel boring.

One of the biggest misconceptions athletes have about investing is that aggression equals success. In sports, effort and intensity matter. In investing, effort does not change outcomes the same way. Process matters more than passion. Discipline matters more than excitement.

Great golfers know when to swing aggressively and when to take something off. They understand that swinging harder does not guarantee better results. Financially, chasing returns often leads to disappointment. Constructing the shot properly leads to steadier progress.

Another key lesson in this section is ownership.

In golf, you own the shot once you hit it. Blaming conditions or equipment does not change the result. Investing demands the same responsibility. Understanding what you own, why you own it, and how it fits into the bigger picture matters more than short-term performance.

This part of the book breaks investing into understandable pieces. How markets function. How different assets behave. How risk and return are connected. How diversification reduces damage. How compounding works over time. These ideas are not complicated, but they are often explained poorly.

The goal here is not to turn you into a trader.

It is to help you think like a disciplined player who respects the course. A player who builds a round by stacking good decisions. A player who avoids forcing shots and trusts a plan that works over time.

Investing is not a one-hole game. It is a season-long strategy.

There will be bad shots. There will be stretches where nothing seems to happen. There will be moments where doing nothing is the hardest decision. Golfers understand this frustration. They also understand that abandoning fundamentals rarely fixes it.

Part III gives you the framework to construct smart financial shots under any conditions. When the foundation is right, you do not need to guess. You choose the shot, commit, and live with the result.

High-percentage shots beat heroic swings in golf.

They win financially too.

Chapter 9: How Financial Markets Really Work

Every golfer eventually realizes the course is alive.

Conditions change. Wind shifts. Greens firm up. What worked yesterday may not work today. The best players do not fight this reality. They learn how the course behaves over time and adjust their strategy without panic. They stop blaming the course and start respecting it.

Financial markets work the same way.

Most frustration with investing comes from misunderstanding how markets actually function. People expect straight lines, predictable outcomes, and immediate feedback. Markets do not operate that way. They move in cycles. They react to countless variables. They reward patience and punish impatience.

This chapter is about understanding the course you are playing on so you stop being surprised by normal conditions.

How markets function

At their core, financial markets exist to connect people who need capital with people who have capital.

Businesses raise money to grow. Investors provide that money in exchange for ownership or interest. Prices move based on expectations about the future. Earnings. Innovation. Risk. Confidence. Fear. All of it shows up in prices.

Markets are not casinos.

They are mechanisms for allocating capital. Over short periods, emotion dominates. Over long periods, fundamentals matter. Golfers understand this difference instinctively. One bad bounce can ruin a hole. Over eighteen holes, skill and decision-making usually win.

Markets reflect collective behavior. Millions of participants buying and selling based on information, beliefs, and emotions. That collective action creates volatility. Volatility is not a flaw. It is a feature.

Expecting markets to be calm all the time is like expecting a course to play the same every day. Weather changes. So do markets.

Stocks, bonds, and ownership

Stocks represent ownership.

When you own stock, you own a piece of a business. You participate in its success and share its risk. That ownership can grow in value and may provide income through dividends. Over time, stock returns are driven by business performance, not headlines.

Bonds represent lending.

When you own a bond, you are lending money to a company or government. In return, you receive interest and the promise of repayment. Bonds are generally less volatile than stocks but offer lower long-term returns.

Ownership and lending serve different roles.

In golf terms, stocks are aggressive clubs used for distance. Bonds are control clubs used for stability. A complete bag includes both. Using only one limits your options.

Many athletes misunderstand stocks because they focus on price movement instead of ownership. Watching prices daily creates emotional reactions. Understanding ownership reframes investing as participation in long-term growth.

Market cycles and volatility

Markets move in cycles.

Expansion. Contraction. Recovery. Repeat. These cycles are normal. They have always existed. They will continue to exist. Trying to predict them precisely is like trying to predict every bounce on a course.

Volatility is simply movement.

It feels uncomfortable because humans prefer certainty. Golfers feel this when conditions get tough. Windy days expose weaknesses. Calm days hide them. Markets do the same thing.

Volatility does not equal loss unless you turn it into one.

Selling during downturns locks in damage. Staying disciplined allows recovery. History consistently shows that markets reward those who stay invested through cycles rather than those who try to jump in and out.

Golfers who abandon their swing every time conditions change never improve. Investors who abandon strategy during volatility experience the same problem.

Long-term strategy vs chasing hot streaks

Every golfer has seen someone get hot for a few holes.

Everything goes in. Shots find fairways. Confidence skyrockets. Then reality returns. Golfers know better than to rebuild their entire game around a short streak.

Investing has hot streaks too.

A stock surges. A sector dominates headlines. Everyone starts talking about easy money. Chasing these streaks feels tempting. It rarely ends well.

Long-term strategy is boring on purpose.

It focuses on asset allocation, diversification, and consistency. It assumes markets will rise over time but fluctuate along the way. It does not rely on timing perfection or insider knowledge.

Chasing hot streaks is emotional investing.

It is reacting instead of planning. It is swinging harder instead of swinging smarter. Over time, it increases risk and reduces returns.

Great golfers trust their process even when others seem to be scoring faster temporarily. Financial success requires the same confidence.

Game situations and decision points

Imagine you are playing a course you know well.

The wind picks up unexpectedly. Do you change your entire swing, or do you adjust club selection and targets?

Markets test investors the same way. Strategy should adapt, not disappear.

Another scenario.

A playing partner is on fire. Do you abandon your plan to keep up, or do you stick to your game?

Comparison destroys discipline. In golf and in money.

Common athlete mistakes and financial parallels

One mistake is expecting immediate results. Golf improvement takes time. Investing rewards patience.

Another mistake is overconfidence after short-term success. A few good holes do not define a season. A few good trades do not define a strategy.

A third mistake is avoiding education. Understanding how markets work reduces fear and improves decisions.

Winning the long game

Markets are not designed to make you comfortable. They are designed to allocate capital efficiently over time.

Great investors, like great golfers, accept variability. They focus on fundamentals. They trust a plan built for the long run.

Once you understand how markets really work, volatility stops feeling like a threat and starts feeling like weather. Something to respect, not fear.

Athlete Takeaways

- Markets are courses, not casinos
- Stocks mean ownership, bonds mean lending
- Volatility is normal, not a warning sign
- Cycles reward patience and punish panic
- Long-term strategy beats chasing hot streaks every time

Chapter 10: Risk, Return, and the Power of Compounding

Every golfer learns this lesson eventually.

Distance matters, but control matters more.

You can swing as hard as you want, but if you lose balance, miss the fairway, or bring hazards into play, the extra yards do not help. The longest hitters in the world still care deeply about dispersion, consistency, and positioning. They understand the tradeoff. More upside usually comes with more risk.

Money works the same way.

Risk and return are always connected. You do not get higher potential returns without accepting more uncertainty. The problem is that many people misunderstand what risk actually is and how it shows up over time. They confuse temporary discomfort with permanent damage. They underestimate the quiet power of compounding. And they wait too long to start.

This chapter is about understanding those tradeoffs clearly so you can make decisions that support long-term success.

Risk and reward tradeoffs

In golf, there is no free swing.

Every aggressive shot carries downside. Every conservative shot limits upside. The key is choosing the right tradeoff for the situation. A par five might invite aggression. A tight par four with trouble everywhere demands restraint.

Financial decisions follow the same logic.

Assets with higher expected returns come with higher variability. Stocks fluctuate more than bonds. Concentrated bets fluctuate more than diversified portfolios. Short-term speculation fluctuates more than long-term ownership.

There is nothing wrong with taking risk. The mistake is taking risk without understanding why.

Risk should be intentional. It should align with your goals, your time horizon, and your ability to stay disciplined when conditions get uncomfortable. Golfers do not attack every pin just because they can. They attack when the odds make sense.

Higher potential reward is earned by accepting uncertainty, not by ignoring it.

Volatility vs permanent loss

This is one of the most important distinctions in investing.

Volatility is movement. Prices go up and down. Accounts fluctuate. Statements look different from month to month. This is normal. It feels uncomfortable, especially when numbers move quickly, but volatility by itself is not loss.

Permanent loss is different.

Permanent loss happens when capital is destroyed or when decisions lock in damage. Selling long-term investments during downturns. Taking on excessive debt that limits flexibility. Investing money needed soon into volatile assets.

Golfers understand this difference instinctively.

A bad bounce is volatility. A ball hit out of bounds is permanent loss. You can recover from discomfort. You cannot recover a stroke that is already gone.

Many athletes panic during normal market swings because they have not been taught this distinction. They react emotionally to volatility and turn temporary movement into permanent damage.

The goal is not to eliminate volatility. The goal is to avoid irreversible mistakes.

Compounding over time

Compounding is the quiet engine of financial success.

It is not exciting. It does not feel dramatic. It works slowly, then all at once. Compounding happens when returns build on top of previous returns, creating exponential growth over time.

Golf has a version of this too.

Small improvements compound. Better fundamentals lead to more fairways. More fairways lead to better approach shots. Better approaches lead to more birdie chances. The gains stack.

Financially, compounding rewards consistency. Regular saving. Long-term investing. Staying invested through cycles. The earlier compounding starts, the more powerful it becomes.

Time matters more than intensity.

Someone who starts early with modest contributions often outperforms someone who starts later with larger contributions. This surprises people because they underestimate the power of time.

Compounding does not require perfection. It requires participation.

The cost of waiting

Waiting feels safe.

In golf, waiting might mean not committing to a swing because you are unsure. That hesitation often leads to poor contact. Financially, waiting often comes from fear of making a mistake. People delay investing because markets feel uncertain, timing feels unclear, or they want more confidence.

The cost of waiting is invisible but real.

Every year spent on the sidelines is a year compounding cannot work for you. Even small delays reduce long-term outcomes dramatically. The damage does not show up immediately, which makes it easy to ignore.

Golfers know this lesson well.

Waiting to practice does not keep skills sharp. Waiting to fix fundamentals allows bad habits to harden. The same is true with money.

You do not need perfect conditions to start. You need a plan and the discipline to follow it.

Game situations and decision points

Imagine this scenario.

You are standing over a shot with a comfortable yardage. The swing feels good. You hesitate because the wind might change. Do you back off every time conditions are not perfect?

Financially, this mirrors waiting for the perfect time to invest. Perfect conditions rarely arrive.

Another scenario.

You experience a bad hole. Do you abandon the round, or do you trust that eighteen holes give you time to recover?

Market downturns test the same mindset. Discipline matters most when conditions are hardest.

Common athlete mistakes and financial parallels

One common mistake is equating risk with danger. In reality, unmanaged risk is dangerous. Managed risk is necessary.

Another mistake is chasing upside without respecting downside. Golfers who swing only for distance lose control. Investors who chase returns lose discipline.

A third mistake is underestimating time. Athletes know seasons are long. Financial success requires the same patience.

Winning the long game

Risk and return are inseparable. Volatility is unavoidable. Compounding is powerful. Waiting is costly.

Great golfers accept tradeoffs. They choose shots they can repeat. They trust that steady progress beats occasional brilliance.

Financial success is built the same way.

You do not need heroic swings. You need smart decisions made consistently over time.

Athlete Takeaways

- Upside always comes with tradeoffs
- Volatility is discomfort, permanent loss is damage
- Compounding rewards consistency, not perfection
- Time matters more than intensity
- Waiting feels safe but quietly costs you the most

Chapter 11: Stocks Without the Highlight Swing

Every golfer loves the highlight swing.

The full send. The high launch. The ball that carries forever and draws applause. It looks powerful. It feels dominant. It also creates expectations that are hard to meet hole after hole. Great golfers enjoy those moments, but they do not build their entire game around them.

Smart investing in stocks works the same way.

Stocks are often marketed like highlight swings. Big winners. Overnight success. Stories of people who picked the right company at the right time. Those stories are real, but they are not representative. Building wealth with stocks is not about swinging for highlights. It is about owning productive businesses and letting time do the work.

This chapter is about understanding stocks for what they actually are and how to use them without letting excitement turn into mistakes.

What owning stock actually means

Owning stock means owning a piece of a business.

It does not mean predicting price movement. It does not mean guessing what will be popular next year. It means you participate in the success or failure of real companies that sell products, hire people, generate profits, and reinvest for growth.

When you buy a stock, you are not buying a lottery ticket. You are buying ownership. That ownership has value because the business produces cash flow over time. Stock prices move because expectations about that future change, but the foundation is business performance.

Many athletes struggle with this idea because stock prices are quoted constantly. Watching prices creates the illusion that investing is about motion. Golfers know better. A swing can look smooth and still produce a poor result. What matters is contact and direction, not appearance.

Focusing on ownership changes behavior. You stop reacting to daily noise. You start asking better questions. What does this company do. How does it make money. Is it likely to still matter years from now.

Ownership thinking reduces emotional swings and encourages patience.

Growth vs value investing

Growth and value are two common ways people describe stocks.

Growth companies are expected to expand faster than the overall market. They reinvest profits, pursue innovation, and often trade at higher prices relative to current earnings. These stocks can produce strong returns, but they can also be volatile because expectations are high.

Value companies are often established businesses trading at lower prices relative to earnings or assets. They may grow more slowly, but they often generate steady cash flow and may pay dividends. These stocks tend to be less volatile but may feel less exciting.

Neither approach is superior all the time.

In golf terms, growth investing is like attacking long par fives. Value investing is like playing steady par fours well. Both contribute to a good round. Problems arise when you insist on only one style regardless of conditions.

Markets rotate. Sometimes growth leads. Sometimes value leads. Trying to time those shifts is difficult. A balanced approach reduces the need to guess.

Many investors get into trouble by chasing whichever style has performed well recently. Golfers know this trap. Just because driver worked on the last hole does not mean it is the right club now.

Dividends and total return

Dividends are cash payments companies make to shareholders.

They represent real money returned to owners. Dividends can be reinvested to buy more shares or used as income. Either way, they are part of the return from owning stock.

Total return is what actually matters.

Total return includes price appreciation plus dividends. Focusing only on price ignores a large part of how stocks create value. Many long-term returns come from reinvested dividends compounding over time.

Golfers understand this concept intuitively.

A round is not defined by one great hole. It is defined by cumulative scoring. Steady pars matter. Small gains add up.

Dividends may not feel exciting, but they create discipline. They reward patience. They provide tangible progress even when prices fluctuate.

Common investing myths

There are several myths that repeatedly cause problems for athletes and investors.

One myth is that you need to pick the right stock to succeed. In reality, diversification matters more than selection. Owning many businesses reduces the impact of any single mistake.

Another myth is that investing requires constant action. Golfers know constant swing changes destroy consistency. Investing works better with fewer, more intentional decisions.

A third myth is that stocks are only for aggressive investors. Stocks are tools. How risky they are depends on how they are used, how diversified they are, and how long they are held.

Another common myth is that past performance guarantees future success. Golfers see this all the time. A hot round yesterday does not guarantee anything today. Markets behave the same way.

Game situations and decision points

Imagine this scenario.

You are playing well and feel confident. Do you start swinging harder on every shot, or do you stay within yourself and protect position?

Financially, this is what happens after strong market performance. Confidence can turn into overexposure if discipline fades.

Another scenario.

You experience a bad stretch. Shots are not falling. Do you abandon fundamentals, or do you trust that process will eventually show up?

Market downturns test the same mindset. Panic turns volatility into permanent loss.

Common athlete mistakes and financial parallels

Athletes often confuse activity with progress. In investing, more trades do not equal better results.

Another mistake is overconfidence. A few good outcomes create the illusion of skill. Golf humbles that quickly. Markets do too.

A third mistake is ignoring the boring parts. Fundamentals win. Flash fades.

Winning the long game

Stocks reward ownership, patience, and discipline.

You do not need highlight swings to build wealth. You need a repeatable approach. You need diversification. You need time.

Great golfers know the round is won by stacking good shots, not by chasing moments.

Stocks work the same way.

Athlete Takeaways

- Owning stock means owning real businesses
- Highlight swings look good but consistency wins
- Growth and value both matter over a full round
- Dividends are steady pars that add up
- Ignore myths and trust a repeatable process

Chapter 12: Bonds and Playing the Long Fairway

Every golfer eventually learns to appreciate the long fairway.

It is not glamorous. It does not create highlight reels. But when pressure rises, the long fairway is where rounds are saved. You aim for the widest landing area, keep the ball in play, and give yourself a manageable next shot. It is disciplined golf. And disciplined golf wins over time.

Bonds play that role in a financial portfolio.

They are not designed to impress. They are designed to stabilize. When stocks feel like aggressive lines over trouble, bonds are the long fairway that keeps you in position. Understanding how bonds work helps you build a portfolio that can handle different conditions without forcing swings.

How bonds work

At their simplest, bonds are loans.

When you buy a bond, you are lending money to a government, municipality, or company. In return, you receive interest payments and the promise that your principal will be returned at maturity. That agreement is the entire structure.

This is different from stocks.

Stocks represent ownership. Bonds represent lending. Owners benefit from growth. Lenders benefit from stability and predictable payments.

In golf terms, buying a bond is choosing control over distance. You know what the shot is designed to do. You are not expecting fireworks. You are expecting reliability.

Bonds typically pay interest at regular intervals. That interest can provide income or be reinvested. When the bond matures, you receive the original amount back, assuming the borrower does not default.

That predictability is the value.

Interest rate and credit risk

Bonds come with two primary risks.

The first is interest rate risk.

When interest rates rise, existing bonds with lower rates become less attractive, and their prices fall. When rates fall, existing bonds become more valuable. This price movement can surprise people who assume bonds never fluctuate.

Golfers understand this concept intuitively.

A shot that was perfect in calm conditions may be wrong when the wind picks up. Conditions change. Equipment does not. Bond prices respond to changing environments the same way.

The second risk is credit risk.

Credit risk is the chance that the borrower cannot make interest payments or return principal. Government bonds are generally considered lower risk. Corporate bonds vary depending on the financial health of the company. Higher risk bonds pay higher interest to compensate for that risk.

This mirrors golf strategy perfectly.

Riskier lines can create higher reward but bring trouble into play. Safer lines reduce downside but limit upside. Bonds exist across a spectrum of risk and return.

Understanding these risks prevents false assumptions. Bonds are not risk-free. They are risk-managed.

When bonds make sense

Bonds make sense when stability matters.

They play an important role when money has a defined time horizon or when volatility would cause emotional stress. Bonds help smooth the ride so investors can stay disciplined through market swings.

Early in a career, investors may lean heavily toward stocks because time is on their side. As goals approach, or responsibilities increase, bonds often become more valuable. They reduce volatility and preserve progress.

This is not about age alone.

It is about purpose. Money needed soon should not take the same risk as money meant for decades of growth. Bonds help align risk with timing.

In golf, you do not attack every hole the same way. Context matters. Bond allocation should change as conditions and objectives change.

Stability in a diversified portfolio

Diversification is about combining different behaviors.

Stocks and bonds behave differently under stress. When stocks struggle, bonds often hold up better. When stocks soar, bonds may lag. That difference creates balance.

Think of it as shot selection across a round.

You use different clubs for different situations. You do not carry twelve drivers. You carry tools that work together.

Bonds help reduce large swings in portfolio value. That reduction in volatility is not just mathematical. It is psychological. When investors experience smaller drawdowns, they are less likely to panic and abandon their plan.

Behavior matters more than precision.

A slightly lower return achieved consistently often beats a higher theoretical return that cannot be tolerated emotionally.

Bonds make discipline easier.

Game situations and decision points

Imagine standing on a long par four with trouble everywhere.

You could try to cut the corner for a shorter approach, or you could aim center fairway and accept a longer shot in. The smarter play depends on your position, confidence, and what the round requires.

Financially, bonds serve that same decision.

Do you need growth right now, or do you need stability so you can stay invested?

Another scenario.

Markets have been volatile, and anxiety is rising. Do you abandon your plan, or do you rely on a portfolio built to handle stress?

Bonds exist to answer that question before it is asked.

Common athlete mistakes and financial parallels

One mistake is assuming bonds are pointless because they do not excite. Golfers who ignore course management often regret it later.

Another mistake is thinking bonds never lose value. They can fluctuate. Understanding risk prevents overreaction.

A third mistake is waiting too long to add stability. Confidence during good conditions hides risk. Preparation matters most before trouble arrives.

Winning the long game

Bonds are not about maximizing returns.

They are about maximizing the chance you stay committed to your strategy through every season. They keep you in the fairway. They reduce damage. They make recovery easier when conditions turn.

Great golfers respect the long fairway.

Great investors respect the role bonds play in long-term success.

Athlete Takeaways

- Bonds are control shots, not highlight swings
- Lending provides stability, not excitement
- Interest rate and credit risk are the hazards to respect
- Bonds help match risk to time horizon
- Staying in the fairway keeps you in the tournament

Chapter 13: Funds, ETFs, and Team Golf Investing

No golfer wins consistently playing alone.

Even individual sports rely on teams. Coaches. Caddies. Trainers. Practice partners. Equipment specialists. Film review. Strength staff. The scoreboard may list one name, but success is built through coordinated effort. Golf looks solitary, but great performance is rarely a solo act.

Investing works the same way.

Trying to win financially by picking a handful of individual stocks is like trying to win a tournament by hitting only hero shots. It can work for a moment, but it rarely holds up over a full season. Funds and ETFs exist to bring team concepts into investing. They spread responsibility, reduce risk, and allow you to benefit from collective performance instead of individual guesses.

This chapter is about understanding how team investing works and why simplicity often outperforms complexity.

Mutual funds vs ETFs

Mutual funds and ETFs are both collections of investments pooled together.

When you invest in either one, you are buying a basket of stocks, bonds, or other assets instead of a single holding. This immediately reduces risk because no one company or issuer determines your outcome.

The difference is mostly about structure and mechanics.

Mutual funds are priced once per day after the market closes. You buy and sell at that end-of-day price. Many mutual funds allow automatic contributions, which makes them useful for long-term investing through retirement plans.

ETFs trade throughout the day like stocks. Prices move continuously. They often have lower minimums and are typically more tax-efficient in taxable accounts. ETFs also tend to be transparent, showing holdings clearly.

Neither is inherently better.

The right choice depends on how you invest, where the account is held, and how much flexibility you want. Golfers understand this intuitively. Some tools work better in practice. Others work better in competition. The goal is function, not status.

The mistake is focusing on the label instead of the purpose. Mutual funds and ETFs are tools. How you use them matters more than which one you choose.

Index vs active strategies

This is one of the most debated topics in investing.

Index strategies aim to match the performance of a market segment. They do not try to outguess the market. They accept market returns at low cost. Active strategies attempt to outperform by selecting securities, timing moves, or adjusting allocations.

In golf terms, index investing is playing the course as designed. Active investing is trying to outplay it.

Both approaches can exist in a portfolio, but understanding tradeoffs matters.

Index strategies are consistent. They are rules-based. They do not rely on individual brilliance. Over time, low costs and broad exposure compound quietly. Many investors underestimate how powerful this simplicity is.

Active strategies can succeed, but they require skill, discipline, and patience. Many underperform due to higher costs, poor timing, or overconfidence.

Golfers know this trap well. Everyone believes they can hit the tough shot until the rough proves otherwise.

For most investors, especially those balancing careers and families, index strategies provide a strong foundation. They reduce decision fatigue and remove the pressure to constantly be right.

Fees and expense ratios

Fees are the strokes you never see until the round is over.

They feel small. They look insignificant. Over time, they add up quietly and permanently. Expense ratios represent the annual cost of running a fund. A fraction of a percent may not seem meaningful, but compounded over decades, it can dramatically reduce outcomes.

Golfers understand this concept through inefficiency.

A swing flaw that costs a yard or two per shot does not feel dramatic. Over eighteen holes, it adds strokes. Over a season, it matters a lot.

High fees create a headwind. Even good performance struggles to overcome them. Lower fees allow more of the return to stay with you.

This does not mean all higher-fee strategies are bad. It means fees must be justified. Paying more should deliver something tangible and consistent. Hope is not a strategy.

Understanding fees is not about being cheap. It is about being intentional.

Diversification without complexity

Diversification is risk management.

It spreads exposure across many assets so no single outcome dominates results. Funds and ETFs make diversification accessible without requiring dozens of individual decisions.

Complexity often feels sophisticated, but it usually creates confusion.

Many athletes fall into the trap of overcomplicating investing. Too many funds. Overlapping holdings. No clear purpose. This mirrors golfers who carry too many swing thoughts and lose rhythm.

Simple portfolios often outperform complicated ones because they are easier to maintain. Easier to rebalance. Easier to stay committed to during stress.

Diversification does not require owning everything. It requires owning enough.

A well-constructed portfolio uses a few broad funds to cover major asset classes. Stocks. Bonds. Domestic. International. The exact mix depends on goals and risk tolerance, not trends.

Team golf investing means trusting structure over impulse.

Game situations and decision points

Imagine this scenario.

You are paired with players who keep trying to outdrive each other. They hit impressive shots but struggle with consistency. Do you abandon your game plan to keep up, or do you trust your steady approach?

Financially, this is the temptation to chase performance. Funds help remove that temptation by focusing on collective outcomes.

Another scenario.

Markets are volatile. Headlines are loud. Do you reshuffle everything, or do you rely on a diversified structure built for these moments?

Team strategies hold up when individual confidence wavers.

Common athlete mistakes and financial parallels

One common mistake is mistaking complexity for intelligence. Golfers know simple swings often win.

Another mistake is ignoring fees because they feel abstract. Abstract costs are still real.

A third mistake is constant tinkering. Changing strategy too often breaks compounding and increases stress.

Athletes who succeed trust systems. They show up. They execute. They let results unfold.

Winning the long game

Funds and ETFs allow investors to stop guessing and start participating.

They bring team concepts into a solo financial game. They reduce reliance on timing. They reward patience. They make discipline easier.

You do not need to know every player on the team. You need to trust the system that brings them together.

High-percentage investing looks boring. It is supposed to. Boring is repeatable. Repeatable wins over time.

Athlete Takeaways

- Team strategies beat solo hero swings
- Mutual funds and ETFs are tools, not trophies
- Index strategies win through discipline and low cost
- Fees are quiet strokes that add up over time
- Simple diversification makes consistency possible

Chapter 14: Real Estate and Alternative Courses

Every golfer eventually faces a choice that is not on the scorecard. Do you play the course as designed, or do you take a different route entirely? Maybe there is a safer line most players use. Maybe there is an alternate fairway that avoids trouble but adds complexity. Great golfers do not avoid these decisions. They evaluate them carefully and choose based on conditions, skill, and long-term goals.

Real estate and alternative investments are those alternate courses.

They can add value. They can reduce risk when used correctly. They can also create problems when misunderstood or forced into a plan without proper preparation. This chapter is about understanding when these paths make sense and how to approach them without letting complexity overwhelm discipline.

Renting vs owning

Owning a home is often described as a financial milestone.

For some people, it is. For others, renting is the smarter play. There is no universal answer because the decision depends on time horizon, flexibility, cash flow, and lifestyle.

In golf terms, renting is like playing a course with flexible tee boxes. You can move. Adjust. Change conditions without much friction. Owning is like committing to a course long term. You gain familiarity and stability, but you also accept maintenance and responsibility.

Owning a home builds equity over time, but it also ties up capital and adds fixed costs. Property taxes. Insurance. Maintenance. Unexpected repairs. These costs are real and often underestimated.

Renting keeps flexibility high. It allows mobility and predictable expenses. The tradeoff is that you do not build equity in the property itself.

The mistake is assuming one option is always superior.

Buying too early or without financial stability can create stress. Renting too long without saving or investing can slow progress. The right decision aligns with your goals and season of life, not outside pressure.

Golfers understand this. You do not play the back tees just because others do. You play the tees that fit your game.

REITs and indirect ownership

Real estate investment trusts, often called REITs, allow investors to own real estate indirectly.

Instead of buying a property, managing tenants, and handling maintenance, you own shares of a company that owns and manages real estate. These can include apartments, office buildings, warehouses, data centers, or retail properties.

REITs provide access.

They offer diversification, liquidity, and professional management. Many pay regular income. They can be bought and sold like stocks, which adds flexibility.

In golf terms, REITs are like using a club designed for consistency rather than raw power. You still participate in real estate returns, but without the operational burden.

Direct ownership offers control and potential tax advantages, but it also demands time, capital, and tolerance for variability. REITs simplify exposure and reduce complexity.

Neither approach is automatically better. They serve different roles. Understanding those roles prevents frustration.

Alternatives like commodities and private investments

Alternative investments cover a wide range of assets.

Commodities like gold, oil, or agricultural products. Private investments in businesses or funds not traded publicly. Hedge funds. Private equity. These assets often behave differently than stocks and bonds.

That difference is the appeal.

Alternatives can reduce reliance on traditional markets and add diversification. However, they also come with tradeoffs. Less transparency. Higher fees. Less liquidity. More complexity.

In golf terms, alternatives are specialty shots.

They can be useful in specific situations. They can also cause trouble if used without skill. Attempting a specialty shot without practice often leads to mistakes.

Many athletes are drawn to alternatives because they sound sophisticated or exclusive. That mindset creates risk. Exclusivity does not equal quality. Complexity does not equal superiority.

Alternatives should serve a clear purpose. Hedging risk. Enhancing diversification. Supporting long-term strategy. If that purpose is not clear, they do not belong in the bag.

Liquidity and risk considerations

Liquidity is how quickly an investment can be converted to cash without significant loss.

Cash is highly liquid. Public stocks and ETFs are liquid. Real estate and private investments are not. Liquidity matters more than most people realize.

In golf, liquidity is flexibility.

When conditions change, flexibility allows adjustment. When money is locked up, options shrink. Unexpected expenses, career changes, or opportunities require access to capital.

Illiquid investments can perform well on paper while creating stress in real life. That mismatch causes problems.

Risk shows up differently here too.

Real estate risk includes vacancy, maintenance, market shifts, and financing costs. Alternative investments add layers of manager risk, strategy risk, and limited transparency.

These risks are not bad. They just require understanding.

Golfers would never attempt a risky shot without knowing what happens if it goes wrong. Financial decisions deserve the same respect.

Game situations and decision points

Imagine this scenario.

You are playing a course with a tempting shortcut over trouble. It saves distance but removes margin. Do you take it on every round, or only when conditions are right?

Real estate and alternatives should be treated the same way. They are not default choices. They are situational tools.

Another scenario.

You commit too much capital to an illiquid investment and then face an unexpected expense. That is like hitting into a narrow fairway repeatedly with no bailout. Eventually, trouble shows up.

Balance matters.

Common athlete mistakes and financial parallels

One common mistake is assuming ownership equals success. Golfers know possession of equipment does not guarantee performance.

Another mistake is underestimating time and effort. Real estate requires management, even when outsourced.

A third mistake is chasing complexity for status. Sophisticated sounding strategies often hide unnecessary risk.

Athletes succeed when they focus on fundamentals and choose tools that support consistency.

Winning the long game

Real estate and alternative investments can add value when used thoughtfully.

They are not required to build wealth. They are not shortcuts. They are options.

Great golfers expand their shot selection slowly. They master fundamentals before experimenting. Financial success works the same way.

Choose alternate courses only when they fit your game, your goals, and your ability to manage risk. Discipline and clarity matter more than novelty.

Athlete Takeaways

- Alternate courses can help or hurt depending on conditions
- Renting and owning both work when aligned with goals
- REITs offer real estate exposure without operational burden
- Alternatives require purpose, patience, and understanding
- Liquidity equals flexibility when the round gets tough

Part IV: Managing the Round

Championship golfers adjust without panic.

Every golfer has felt the round start to shift.

The swing feels a little off. The wind changes. Putts stop falling. Nothing is falling apart, but nothing feels automatic either. This is the moment that separates good players from great ones. Some panic. They start changing everything. Grip. Tempo. Strategy. Others slow down, make small adjustments, and trust the work they have already done.

Championship golfers adjust without panic.

Managing the round is not about reinvention. It is about awareness, restraint, and confidence. You recognize what is happening, make measured changes, and stay committed to the overall plan. Financial management works the same way.

Most people make their worst money decisions in the middle of the round.

They react to headlines. They chase performance. They abandon strategy during volatility. They overcorrect after a setback. These reactions feel logical in the moment, but they usually create more damage than the original problem.

This section of the book is about learning how to manage money once the foundation is built.

By this point, you understand cash flow, protection, and investing fundamentals. Now the focus shifts to execution. Asset allocation. Buying and holding. Rebalancing. Managing emotions. These are the skills that determine whether a solid plan actually works over time.

In golf, you do not evaluate your swing after every shot.

You collect information. You notice patterns. You adjust when necessary. Over-adjusting creates chaos. Financially, constant tinkering breaks discipline and increases stress. The goal is not activity. The goal is consistency.

Managing the round also means understanding that conditions will change.

Markets go up and down. Life events happen. Income shifts. Goals evolve. A good plan anticipates change and builds in flexibility so adjustments feel controlled instead of desperate.

Another key concept in this section is trust.

Golfers trust their preparation. They trust their routine. They trust that one bad hole does not define the day. Financial success requires the same mindset. Short-term results do not invalidate long-term strategy.

This part of the book focuses on how to position assets appropriately, how to execute trades thoughtfully, how to rebalance without emotion, and how to handle the mental side of money. These chapters emphasize discipline over brilliance.

Championship rounds are rarely flashy from start to finish.

They are steady. Intentional. Composed. The player who wins is often the one who makes the fewest big mistakes, not the one who takes the most risk.

Managing the round financially means knowing when to act and when to stay still. It means trusting your plan enough to let it work. It means adjusting without panic when conditions demand it.

That is how championships are won on the course.

That is how long-term financial success is built too.

Chapter 15: Asset Allocation and Course Positioning

Every golfer knows position matters.

You can hit a great shot that leaves you in the wrong place and suddenly the next shot becomes harder than it should be. You can also hit a conservative shot that leaves you in perfect position and makes the hole feel simple. Championship golf is not just about striking the ball well. It is about putting yourself in spots where the game becomes easier.

Asset allocation is course positioning for money.

It determines how your financial round plays out under different conditions. It influences how much stress you feel during volatility, how likely you are to stick with your plan, and how well your portfolio supports your goals over time. Great allocation does not eliminate risk. It manages it so you can keep playing smart golf financially.

Stocks, bonds, and cash balance

Think of stocks, bonds, and cash as different clubs with different jobs.

Stocks are your distance clubs. They provide growth over time, but they come with variability. Prices move. Statements fluctuate. Over long periods, stocks have rewarded patience, but short-term swings are part of the deal.

Bonds are your control clubs. They smooth the ride. They reduce volatility and provide income or stability. They usually do not grow as fast as stocks, but they help you stay disciplined when markets get uncomfortable.

Cash is your wedge and putter. It does not generate much return, but it provides flexibility. Cash covers short-term needs, emergencies, and planned expenses. It prevents you from being forced to sell long-term investments at bad times.

The balance between these three determines how playable your financial course feels.

Too much stock exposure can make the round emotionally exhausting. Too much cash can slow progress. Too many bonds can limit growth. There is no perfect mix for everyone. The right balance matches your goals, time horizon, and tolerance for variability.

Golfers do not carry all drivers or all wedges. Balance matters.

Domestic vs international exposure

Many investors focus only on what they know.

Domestic stocks feel familiar. The companies are recognizable. The news is constant. That familiarity creates comfort, but comfort can lead to concentration.

International exposure adds diversification.

Companies outside your home country participate in different economic cycles, currencies, and growth patterns. Sometimes domestic markets lead. Sometimes international markets do. Owning both reduces dependence on any single region.

In golf terms, this is like playing only one course your entire career. You might know it well, but your game becomes limited. Playing different courses develops adaptability.

International investing is not about predicting which country will win next year. It is about spreading exposure so no single market defines your outcome.

The goal is not complexity. It is balance.

Diversification principles

Diversification is one of the most misunderstood concepts in investing.

It does not guarantee gains. It does not prevent losses. What it does is reduce the impact of any single mistake or event. It keeps one bad shot from ruining the round.

Diversification works across multiple dimensions. Asset classes. Industries. Regions. Time. Owning many different return sources smooths outcomes and makes discipline easier.

Golfers understand this instinctively.

You do not rely on one shot type for an entire round. You develop a complete game so you can respond to whatever the course demands.

Over-diversification can be a problem too. Owning too many overlapping investments adds complexity without benefit. The goal is thoughtful diversification, not accumulation.

Simple, well-constructed portfolios often outperform complicated ones because they are easier to manage and stick with.

Career-stage allocation

Asset allocation should evolve over time.

Early in a career, time is your biggest advantage. Income may be growing. Expenses may be lower. Volatility is easier to tolerate because goals are far away. Portfolios often lean more heavily toward growth assets.

As careers progress, responsibilities increase. Families. Mortgages. Business interests. Volatility becomes more stressful because mistakes matter more. Allocation often shifts gradually toward stability.

Later in life, preserving progress becomes a priority. Income generation and risk management matter more than aggressive growth. Allocation reflects that reality.

This progression is not automatic or strictly age-based.

Career stability, income predictability, and personal comfort all matter. A stable professional with strong cash flow may tolerate more risk than someone with variable income, regardless of age.

Golfers make similar adjustments.

Early in a round, you may play more aggressively. As the round unfolds and position matters more, strategy shifts. That does not mean fear. It means intelligence.

Game situations and decision points

Imagine this scenario.

You are leading late in a tournament. Do you start firing at every pin, or do you play center green and protect the lead?

Financially, this mirrors late-career allocation decisions. Preserving position matters.

Another scenario.

You are early in the round with plenty of holes left. Do you play scared, or do you take calculated risks to build momentum?

Early investing years allow for more aggressive positioning. Understanding where you are in the round guides decisions.

A third scenario.

Markets drop sharply. Your allocation suddenly feels uncomfortable. Do you abandon the plan, or do you recognize that discomfort is part of the design?

Proper allocation anticipates volatility so it does not feel like a surprise.

Common athlete mistakes and financial parallels

One common mistake is copying someone else's setup.

Golfers know this well. Using someone else's clubs or swing rarely works. Financially, copying allocation without understanding context leads to regret.

Another mistake is never adjusting.

Setups that worked years ago may no longer fit current conditions. Review matters. Adjustment does not mean overhaul.

A third mistake is equating risk tolerance with bravery.

Risk tolerance is not toughness. It is honesty about how you respond under pressure. Ignoring that truth leads to poor decisions when stress hits.

Winning the long game

Asset allocation is not about predicting markets.

It is about building a portfolio that lets you stay disciplined across seasons. It positions you for growth without exposing you to unnecessary damage. It turns investing from an emotional experience into a strategic one.

Great golfers care deeply about position.

They choose shots that make the next decision easier. Financial success works the same way. When your assets are positioned correctly, you do not need to guess or panic. You manage the round.

That is how championships are won.

Athlete Takeaways

- Position matters more than power
- Balance stocks, bonds, and cash intentionally
- Diversification keeps one bad shot from ending the round
- Adjust allocation as your career and responsibilities change
- Build a setup you can trust under pressure

Chapter 16: Buying, Holding, and Trusting Your Swing

Every golfer has stood over a shot thinking too much.

You replay mechanics. You second-guess club choice. You feel the pressure of the moment. Then the swing breaks down, not because you lack skill, but because you stopped trusting it. The best players commit. They pick the shot, trust their preparation, and swing.

Investing demands the same confidence.

Buying, holding, and trusting your swing financially is not about being reckless. It is about executing a plan with discipline and resisting the urge to interfere when emotions get loud. This chapter is about how to enter the market thoughtfully, how to place trades intelligently, and how to stay invested when doubt shows up.

Opening and funding accounts

Before you ever buy an investment, the setup matters.

In golf, setup determines everything. Grip, stance, alignment. Financially, setup means having the right accounts opened and funded correctly. Brokerage accounts for taxable investing. Retirement accounts for long-term goals. Each account has a role, and mixing them carelessly creates confusion.

Opening accounts is straightforward. The harder part is funding them consistently.

Many athletes wait for perfect timing or excess cash. That usually means nothing happens. Smart golfers do not wait for perfect conditions to practice. They show up and take reps. Funding accounts regularly turns intention into progress.

Automatic contributions remove hesitation. They reduce the temptation to time the market. They make investing routine instead of dramatic. Routine is your friend.

The goal is not to time the first purchase perfectly. The goal is to build a habit that compounds over time.

Market orders vs limit orders

How you place trades matters more than people realize.

A market order buys or sells immediately at the best available price. It prioritizes execution. A limit order sets a specific price and waits for the market to meet it. It prioritizes price.

Both tools have value.

Market orders are simple. They work well for long-term investing where small price differences do not matter. Limit orders can make sense when markets are volatile or when trading less liquid investments.

The mistake is overthinking execution.

Many investors obsess over getting the perfect price and miss the opportunity to invest altogether. Golfers know this trap. Waiting for perfect conditions often leads to indecision and poor swings.

Execution matters. Perfection does not.

For long-term investors, getting invested consistently matters more than shaving pennies off entry prices.

Buy-and-hold discipline

Buy-and-hold is not laziness. It is discipline.

It means buying investments aligned with your strategy and holding them through normal market ups and downs. It accepts volatility as part of the process. It relies on time, not timing.

Golfers understand this mindset deeply.

You do not abandon your swing after one bad hole. You trust that fundamentals hold up over eighteen holes. Financially, buy-and-hold trusts that markets reward patience over years and decades.

The hardest part of buy-and-hold is not buying. It is holding.

Holding during market downturns tests confidence. Statements shrink. Headlines get loud. Friends start talking about selling. This is where most investors fail, not because the strategy is wrong, but because emotion takes over.

Buy-and-hold works because it removes the need to guess. It avoids the trap of trying to predict short-term movements. It allows compounding to do its job uninterrupted.

Avoiding emotional decisions

Emotion is the biggest enemy of good investing.

Fear shows up during downturns. Greed shows up during rallies. Comparison shows up constantly. These emotions push people to make decisions that feel urgent but are rarely thoughtful.

Golfers experience the same thing.

A bad shot creates frustration. A great shot creates overconfidence. The player who reacts emotionally loses rhythm. The player who stays composed stays competitive.

Financial discipline requires the same restraint.

One of the most effective ways to avoid emotional decisions is to reduce how often you look. Constant checking amplifies noise. Noise fuels reaction. Reaction breaks strategy.

Another tool is having clear rules.

Know why you own what you own. Know under what circumstances you would change course. If those circumstances are not met, do nothing. Doing nothing is often the hardest and smartest move.

Structure protects you from yourself.

Game situations and decision points

Imagine this situation.

You are mid-round. The swing feels slightly off. Do you rebuild everything on the spot, or do you make a small adjustment and trust your base?

Financially, this is what happens during market volatility. Small adjustments may be appropriate. Overhauls are rarely wise.

Another scenario.

You hit a great shot and feel unstoppable. Do you start swinging harder, or do you stay within your routine?

Strong markets create the same temptation. Confidence can turn into recklessness if discipline fades.

A third scenario.

You see others making moves and talking confidently. Do you abandon your plan to keep up?

Comparison destroys trust. Your swing is your swing. Your plan is your plan.

Common athlete mistakes and financial parallels

One common mistake is equating action with improvement. In golf, too many swing thoughts ruin tempo. In investing, too many trades ruin results.

Another mistake is changing strategy based on short-term outcomes. A few holes do not define a round. A few months do not define an investment plan.

A third mistake is abandoning structure during stress. Stress is when structure matters most.

Athletes who succeed trust systems. They commit. They execute. They accept outcomes without panic.

Winning the long game

Buying and holding is not about stubbornness.

It is about understanding that progress happens quietly when discipline stays intact. It is about trusting preparation. It is about knowing that one bad stretch does not invalidate the plan.

Great golfers trust their swing under pressure.

Great investors trust their strategy when emotions rise.

When you buy thoughtfully, hold patiently, and avoid emotional decisions, investing stops feeling chaotic. It becomes boring in the best way. Predictable. Manageable. Effective.

That is how championships are won over time.

Athlete Takeaways

- Commit to the shot and trust your preparation
- Consistent funding beats perfect timing
- Execution matters more than entry price
- Buy-and-hold requires discipline, not passivity
- Emotion ruins swings and investment results

Chapter 17: Rebalancing and Momentum Shifts

Every golfer knows momentum is real.

You string together a few good holes and everything feels easier. Timing improves. Confidence rises. Then, without warning, momentum shifts. The swing feels fine, but results change. The mistake many players make is assuming momentum will last forever or trying to force it back when it fades. Championship golfers recognize momentum for what it is. Temporary. Useful. Never permanent.

Rebalancing exists for the same reason.

In investing, momentum shifts constantly. Markets move. Asset classes drift. What started balanced slowly becomes tilted. Rebalancing is how you bring the portfolio back into position without panic, ego, or overreaction. It is course management in the middle of the round.

How often to review investments

In golf, you do not check the scorecard after every shot.

You glance at it periodically to stay aware, not to obsess. Financial reviews should work the same way. Reviewing too often increases noise and emotion. Reviewing too rarely allows drift to go unnoticed.

For most long-term investors, periodic reviews are enough.

Quarterly or semiannual check-ins are usually sufficient. Annual reviews are essential. These moments are about assessment, not action. You are asking simple questions. Has anything drifted meaningfully. Has my situation changed. Does the plan still match reality.

Constant monitoring creates false urgency. Markets move every day, but daily movement rarely requires action. Golfers know this instinctively. One bad swing does not require a rebuild.

Reviews create awareness. Awareness prevents surprise. Surprise causes panic.

Rebalancing strategies

Rebalancing is the act of restoring your portfolio to its intended mix.

Over time, assets that perform well grow faster and take up more space. Assets that lag shrink. Without intervention, risk increases quietly. Rebalancing trims what has grown and adds to what has lagged.

This feels counterintuitive emotionally.

You are selling what feels good and buying what feels disappointing. Golfers experience this too. When one club is working, you want to keep using it. When another is struggling, you want to avoid it. Smart players stick to strategy.

There are several ways to rebalance.

Time-based rebalancing happens on a schedule. Once or twice a year, you bring things back to target regardless of market conditions. This is simple and disciplined.

Threshold-based rebalancing happens when allocations drift beyond a certain range. For example, if stocks move more than a set percentage away from target, adjustments are made. This approach responds to meaningful changes without constant tinkering.

Cash-flow rebalancing uses new contributions to correct drift. Adding money to underweighted assets avoids selling and can be tax efficient.

The specific method matters less than consistency. Rebalancing is not about precision. It is about maintaining discipline over time.

Life changes and portfolio updates

Markets are not the only reason portfolios change.

Life events matter just as much.

New jobs. Income changes. Marriage. Children. Home purchases. Business ownership. Health changes. These events alter risk tolerance, cash needs, and time horizons. Ignoring them creates mismatch.

In golf terms, this is like playing the same strategy regardless of weather or course setup. Conditions change. Strategy must adapt.

Portfolio updates should follow life changes thoughtfully, not emotionally. A raise may allow for higher savings. A new responsibility may call for more stability. A career shift may reduce tolerance for volatility.

These adjustments are strategic, not reactive.

The mistake is making changes based on fear or excitement instead of context. Life changes are signals to review, not reasons to overhaul.

Avoiding over-adjustment

Over-adjustment is one of the most damaging habits in both golf and investing.

In golf, over-adjustment shows up as constant swing thoughts. Fixing one thing creates another problem. Rhythm disappears. Confidence fades.

Financially, over-adjustment looks like frequent reallocations, chasing trends, and abandoning strategy after short-term outcomes. Each move feels justified in isolation. Over time, results suffer.

Markets will always provide reasons to act.

Headlines. Predictions. Opinions. Data. Most of it is noise. Rebalancing provides structure so you do not have to decide constantly. It limits action to moments that actually matter.

Doing less is often doing better.

Championship golfers adjust only when necessary. They trust that small corrections are more effective than dramatic changes. Investors need the same restraint.

Game situations and decision points

Imagine this scenario.

You are mid-round and realize you are playing aggressively because you feel confident. A few holes later, trouble appears. Do you double down on aggression to regain momentum, or do you reset and protect position?

Financially, this is what happens after strong market performance. Rebalancing pulls risk back into line before confidence turns into exposure.

Another scenario.

Markets fall and one part of your portfolio shrinks noticeably. Do you avoid it because it feels uncomfortable, or do you rebalance and restore balance?

This decision separates disciplined investors from reactive ones.

A third scenario.

Your life changes significantly, but your strategy does not. That mismatch quietly increases risk. Reviews exist to catch this early.

Common athlete mistakes and financial parallels

One common mistake is confusing movement with progress. More swings do not equal better golf. More trades do not equal better investing.

Another mistake is reacting to short-term results. Golfers know one hole does not define a round. Investors need the same perspective.

A third mistake is ignoring drift. Small changes compound. Awareness prevents regret.

Athletes who succeed trust systems and respect timing. They adjust deliberately, not emotionally.

Winning the long game

Rebalancing is not exciting.

It is not meant to be. It is meant to work.

It keeps risk aligned. It enforces discipline. It turns momentum into opportunity instead of danger. It allows long-term strategy to survive short-term noise.

Championship golfers adjust without panic.

They notice changes. They make small corrections. They stay committed to the plan.

Financial success requires the same maturity. When you rebalance intentionally, review periodically, and avoid over-adjustment, you stay in control even when momentum shifts.

That is how long rounds are managed. That is how long-term financial success is protected.

Athlete Takeaways

- Momentum is temporary, discipline is permanent
- Review periodically, not obsessively
- Rebalancing trims risk before it becomes damage
- Life changes require strategy check-ins
- Small adjustments beat constant tinkering

Chapter 18: The Mental Side of Money

Every golfer knows the swing is only half the battle.

You can have perfect mechanics and still struggle if your head is not right. Pressure tightens muscles. Confidence frees them. Momentum amplifies everything. The physical game matters, but the mental game decides how well you execute when it counts.

Money is no different.

Most financial mistakes are not caused by lack of knowledge. They are caused by emotion. Fear. Greed. Comparison. Impatience. This chapter is about understanding the mental side of money and learning how to stay composed when pressure shows up.

Pressure, confidence, and momentum

Pressure changes behavior.

In golf, pressure makes the club feel heavier. It speeds up tempo. It causes hesitation or aggression at the wrong moments. Financial pressure creates the same reactions. Bills pile up. Markets drop. Income changes. Decisions feel urgent even when they are not.

Confidence is the antidote.

Golfers who trust their preparation swing freely. Financial confidence comes from structure. Clear cash flow. Emergency savings. Diversified investments. When systems are in place, pressure loses power.

Momentum amplifies emotion.

When things are going well, confidence can turn into overconfidence.

When things go poorly, frustration can turn into panic. Great golfers recognize momentum but do not chase it. Financially, chasing momentum often leads to buying high and selling low.

Understanding momentum helps you avoid letting emotion dictate strategy.

Crowd noise and comparison

Golfers hear crowd noise constantly.

Applause. Groans. Commentary. Other players' reactions. Paying too much attention pulls focus away from your own game. Financially, crowd noise is everywhere. Social media. News headlines. Friends talking about investments. Stories of quick wins.

Comparison is toxic.

It creates urgency where none exists. It makes disciplined strategies feel slow. It pushes people to abandon plans that are working quietly. Golfers know this trap. Playing someone else's game rarely works.

Your financial plan is personal.

Different income. Different goals. Different timelines. Comparing outcomes without context leads to poor decisions.

Reducing noise is a competitive advantage.

Limiting how often you check balances. Choosing reliable information sources. Ignoring predictions and hype. These habits protect focus.

Building systems for discipline

Discipline fades. Systems endure.

Golfers do not rely on motivation to practice. They follow schedules. Routines. Checklists. These systems remove decision-making and protect consistency.

Financial discipline works the same way.

Automation is a system. Automatic savings. Automatic investing. Automatic bill payments. These systems reduce reliance on willpower.

Rules are systems.

Know when you will invest. Know when you will rebalance. Know when you will ignore noise. Write these rules down. When emotions rise, rules take over.

Environment matters too.

If spending is too easy, discipline erodes. If investing requires effort, procrastination wins. Adjust the environment so good behavior is easy and bad behavior is harder.

Staying composed after bad shots

Bad shots happen.

In golf, how you respond matters more than the mistake itself. Getting angry compounds damage. Staying calm allows recovery.

Financial setbacks work the same way.

Unexpected expenses. Market downturns. Missed opportunities. These moments test composure. Panic leads to permanent damage. Calm allows recovery.

One bad decision does not ruin a financial life unless it triggers a series of emotional reactions. Great golfers limit damage. Financially, the same rule applies.

Reflection beats reaction.

Ask what happened. Adjust if needed. Move on. Dwelling does not help.

Game situations and decision points

Imagine this.

You hit a terrible shot early in the round. Do you try to make it back immediately, or do you reset and trust the process?

Financially, this is what happens after losses. Chasing recovery creates more risk.

Another scenario.

Everyone around you is talking about a hot investment. Do you feel pressure to join, or do you stick to your plan?

Crowd noise tests discipline constantly.

A third scenario.

You experience success and feel invincible. Do you abandon caution, or do you stay grounded?

Confidence should reinforce discipline, not replace it.

Common athlete mistakes and financial parallels

One common mistake is emotional overcorrection. Fixing feelings instead of fixing process.

Another mistake is letting ego drive decisions. Ego swings harder than strategy.

A third mistake is confusing activity with control. Doing something feels better than doing nothing, but doing nothing is often correct.

Athletes who succeed mentally build routines and trust them under pressure.

Winning the long game

The mental side of money determines whether good strategies survive stress.

Great golfers stay composed. They respect pressure without fearing it. They focus on the next shot, not the last one.

Financial success requires the same mindset.

When you control emotion, reduce noise, build systems, and stay composed after mistakes, money becomes manageable. The mental game stops sabotaging the plan.

You will never eliminate emotion. You can manage it.

That is how championships are won when the pressure is highest.

Athlete Takeaways

- Pressure reveals discipline, not talent
- Noise and comparison break focus fast
- Systems protect you when motivation fades
- One bad shot only hurts if you let it
- Composure keeps you in the tournament

Part V: The Long Season and Life Beyond the Course

Every golfer eventually realizes the round is only part of the story.

You train for weeks or months to play a few hours. You obsess over mechanics, strategy, and execution, but the majority of life happens off the course. Travel. Recovery. Relationships. Career decisions. Identity. Golf is important, but it is not everything. The same is true with money.

This part of the book is about zooming out.

Up to this point, the focus has been on fundamentals, protection, investing, and managing the round. Those skills matter. They keep you competitive. But long-term success depends on how money fits into the rest of your life, not just how well it performs on paper.

The long season tests different skills.

Early in a career, energy and opportunity are high. Later, responsibilities grow. Priorities shift. Bodies change. Goals evolve. Great golfers adjust expectations and strategy over time instead of clinging to who they used to be. Financial decisions require the same maturity.

Money decisions in this phase are less about optimization and more about alignment.

Taxes matter because they quietly affect outcomes. Retirement planning matters because income eventually needs to replace effort. Housing decisions matter because they shape flexibility. Career choices matter because income is the fuel for everything else. Family conversations matter because money does not exist in isolation.

This is where many people struggle.

They understand investing but avoid conversations. They earn well but fail to plan transitions. They focus on growth while ignoring structure. Over time, these gaps create stress that no portfolio can fix.

Golfers know that ignoring recovery eventually leads to injury. Financially, ignoring life context leads to burnout, conflict, or regret.

This section is designed to help you think beyond the next shot.

It acknowledges that life is not static. Careers change. Families grow. Parents age. Health fluctuates. Opportunities appear unexpectedly. The goal is not to predict everything. The goal is to build flexibility so you can respond without panic.

Another key theme here is intentional decision-making.

Many major financial decisions are made by default. Renewing leases. Accepting job offers without understanding benefits. Buying cars because payments seem manageable. Naming beneficiaries once and never revisiting them. These decisions feel small individually. Over time, they shape outcomes dramatically.

Golfers understand the danger of autopilot.

You stop reading greens carefully. You rush routines. You assume outcomes. That is when mistakes creep in. Financial autopilot works the same way unless it is designed intentionally.

This part of the book also addresses communication.

Money affects families. Partners. Children. Parents. Avoiding conversations does not protect relationships. It strains them. Clear expectations and boundaries matter. Teaching financial habits early matters. Planning for caregiving matters. These topics are uncomfortable, but ignoring them creates bigger problems later.

Life beyond the course also includes identity.

Many athletes struggle with transitions when competition ends or roles change. Money can either amplify that stress or reduce it depending on preparation. Financial stability creates options. Options create confidence. Confidence supports identity beyond performance.

This section is not about perfection.

It is about awareness. Preparation. Honest assessment. The same traits that sustain long athletic careers sustain financial lives as well.

The long season rewards patience, adaptability, and perspective.

Golf teaches that the game is never finished. There is always another round. Another adjustment. Another opportunity to play smarter. Financial life works the same way.

Part V focuses on building a financial life that supports who you are becoming, not just who you have been.

Chapter 19: Taxes and Where You Place Your Shots

Every golfer learns that the target is not always the pin.

Sometimes the smartest play is aiming away from trouble so the ball feeds back to the right spot. The shot may look conservative, but it produces a better result. Great golfers understand that where you aim matters just as much as how you swing.

Taxes work the same way.

Most people think about returns before they think about taxes. They focus on what they earn and forget about what they keep. Taxes are not a separate topic from investing. They are part of the course layout. Ignoring them is like ignoring a bunker guarding the green. You might get away with it for a while, but eventually it costs strokes.

This chapter is about understanding how different accounts are taxed and how placing the right assets in the right accounts can quietly improve long-term results.

Taxable vs tax-advantaged accounts

Not all investment accounts are treated the same.

Taxable accounts are straightforward. You invest money that has already been taxed. When you earn interest, dividends, or capital gains, you may owe taxes along the way. These accounts offer flexibility. You can access money at any time without penalties. The tradeoff is ongoing taxation.

Tax-advantaged accounts are designed to encourage long-term saving.

Retirement accounts, education accounts, and health-related accounts often receive special tax treatment. The government trades flexibility for incentives. If you follow the rules, taxes are reduced or delayed.

In golf terms, taxable accounts are wide fairways with visible hazards. Tax-advantaged accounts are narrower routes with better outcomes if you stay within the lines.

Neither is better in all situations. The right mix depends on goals, time horizon, and flexibility needs. The mistake is treating all accounts the same and hoping it works out.

Tax-deferred vs tax-free growth

Tax-advantaged accounts fall into two main categories.

Tax-deferred growth means you get a deduction or deferral now, but you pay taxes later when money is withdrawn. Traditional retirement accounts work this way. Taxes are postponed while money grows.

Tax-free growth means you pay taxes upfront, but qualified withdrawals later are tax-free. Roth-style accounts work this way.

Both approaches have value.

Tax-deferred growth helps when current income is high and future income may be lower. Tax-free growth helps when future tax rates may be higher or when flexibility matters later in life.

Golfers understand this tradeoff intuitively.

Sometimes you take a longer club now to avoid trouble later. Other times you accept a tougher shot now to set up an easier finish. Tax decisions work the same way. There is no universal right answer. There is only the right answer for your situation.

Mixing tax-deferred and tax-free accounts creates flexibility. Flexibility allows better decision-making later when circumstances change.

Asset location basics

Asset location is about where you place investments, not which investments you choose.

This concept is often overlooked because it feels subtle. It does not change what you own. It changes where you hold it. Over time, that placement affects how much tax you pay.

Some investments generate more taxable income than others. Interest and short-term gains are taxed more heavily. Long-term growth is taxed more favorably. Placing higher-tax investments in tax-advantaged accounts can reduce drag. Placing tax-efficient investments in taxable accounts can preserve flexibility.

In golf terms, this is choosing the right landing areas.

You might hit the same shot shape, but aiming to the right side of the fairway opens the green. Asset location quietly improves outcomes without changing strategy.

This is not about complexity. It is about intention.

A well-located portfolio does not eliminate taxes. It minimizes unnecessary ones. Over decades, that difference compounds meaningfully.

Common tax mistakes

Many tax mistakes are predictable.

One common mistake is ignoring taxes entirely until filing season. That is like adding up the score only after the round is over and being surprised by the result. Awareness throughout the year allows adjustments.

Another mistake is placing investments randomly across accounts. Convenience drives decisions instead of strategy. Over time, this creates inefficiency.

A third mistake is assuming higher returns always mean better outcomes. After-tax returns matter more. A lower return that keeps more money can outperform a higher return that leaks taxes constantly.

Another frequent error is overtrading in taxable accounts. Frequent buying and selling creates taxable events. Activity feels productive. Results suffer.

Finally, many athletes delay learning about taxes because the topic feels overwhelming. Avoidance is costly. Basic understanding goes a long way.

Game situations and decision points

Imagine this situation.

You have a tucked pin behind a bunker. You could aim directly at it, or you could aim center green and two-putt. The aggressive play feels tempting. The smart play protects the scorecard.

Financially, chasing returns without considering tax impact creates the same risk. Smart placement protects progress.

Another scenario.

You have multiple accounts and new money to invest. Do you place it wherever it is easiest, or do you choose intentionally based on tax impact?

Small decisions repeated consistently matter more than one big move.

A third scenario.

You experience a year of unusually high income. Do you ignore tax planning, or do you adjust contributions and timing to reduce damage?

Golfers adapt strategy when conditions change. Taxes demand the same flexibility.

Common athlete mistakes and financial parallels

Athletes often focus on offense. Scoring. Growth. Performance. Defense feels boring. Taxes are financial defense.

Another mistake is procrastination. Delaying decisions feels safe but creates missed opportunities.

A third mistake is relying on hearsay. Tax myths spread easily. Understanding beats assumptions.

Golfers trust yardage books and preparation. Financial decisions deserve the same respect.

Winning the long game

Taxes will always be part of the game.

You cannot eliminate them, but you can manage them. Where you place your shots matters. Intentional account use, thoughtful asset location, and awareness of tax treatment quietly improve outcomes.

Great golfers do not aim at every pin.

Great investors do not ignore taxes.

When you understand how taxable and tax-advantaged accounts work together, money becomes more efficient. The plan becomes more resilient. You keep more of what you earn.

That is not flashy. It is winning golf.

Athlete Takeaways

- The target is not always the pin
- After-tax results matter more than headline returns
- Different accounts have different rules for a reason
- Asset location is quiet course management
- Smart placement saves strokes over time

Chapter 20: Retirement Accounts and Financial Independence

Every golfer eventually thinks beyond the current round.

You are still competing. You still want to play well today. But you also start thinking about longevity. How long your body will hold up. How you want the game to fit into your life years from now. Smart players plan for a future where performance changes but enjoyment and independence remain.

Retirement planning is that long view for money.

It is not about stopping work on a specific birthday. It is about building financial independence so work becomes a choice, not a requirement. Retirement accounts are the tools that make that possible when used correctly.

Employer plans and pensions

Employer-sponsored retirement plans are often the foundation.

401(k) plans, 403(b) plans, and similar programs allow you to save and invest directly from your paycheck. Contributions are automatic, which removes friction and hesitation. Many employers also offer matching contributions. That match is extra compensation. Leaving it unused is like leaving strokes on the course.

Pensions still exist in some fields. They promise income later in life based on years of service and earnings. If you have one, understand it. How it is calculated. When benefits begin. What options exist for survivors. Pensions can be valuable, but they should be integrated into a broader plan, not assumed to be enough on their own.

Employer plans have rules.

Contribution limits exist. Investment menus are limited. Withdrawal restrictions apply. These constraints are not flaws. They are guardrails designed to encourage long-term behavior.

Golfers understand structure.

Practice plans. Training schedules. Team rules. Structure supports consistency. Employer plans do the same thing for saving.

Traditional and Roth IRAs

Individual retirement accounts expand flexibility.

Traditional IRAs allow tax-deferred growth. Contributions may be deductible depending on income and access to employer plans. Taxes are paid later when money is withdrawn.

Roth IRAs flip that equation. Contributions are made with after-tax dollars, but qualified withdrawals are tax-free. This creates powerful flexibility later in life.

Choosing between traditional and Roth options is about timing.

Pay taxes now or later. There is no universally correct answer. Income level. Career trajectory. Tax expectations. Flexibility needs. All of these matter.

Many athletes benefit from a mix.

Diversifying tax treatment is like diversifying clubs. It gives options when conditions change. Later in life, having both tax-deferred and tax-free sources allows smarter income planning.

The mistake is thinking in absolutes.

One account type is rarely sufficient by itself. Balance creates control.

Contribution and withdrawal rules

Retirement accounts reward discipline and punish impatience.

Contribution limits cap how much you can add each year. These limits are not arbitrary. They encourage steady progress rather than short bursts.

Withdrawal rules protect the long-term goal.

Taking money out early often triggers penalties and taxes. Those consequences exist to discourage short-term thinking. Using retirement accounts like checking accounts undermines compounding.

There are exceptions.

Education expenses. First-time home purchases. Medical costs. Understanding these exceptions matters, but relying on them routinely breaks the plan.

Golfers know this lesson well.

You can take aggressive lines occasionally, but building a strategy around exceptions creates inconsistency. Retirement accounts work best when left alone to do their job.

Retirement income basics

Saving for retirement is only half the equation.

The other half is converting savings into income. This transition requires planning. Withdraw too aggressively and money may not last. Withdraw too conservatively and lifestyle suffers unnecessarily.

Retirement income comes from multiple sources.

Employer plans. IRAs. Taxable accounts. Social Security. Possibly pensions. The order and timing of withdrawals affect taxes, flexibility, and longevity.

This is where preparation pays off.

Golfers prepare for closing holes differently than opening holes. Strategy shifts. Financially, income planning is the back nine of the career. Decisions matter more because recovery time is limited.

Income planning focuses on sustainability.

How much can be withdrawn each year. How markets affect income. How inflation erodes purchasing power. These factors must be balanced thoughtfully.

There is no single formula that works for everyone. Flexibility and awareness matter more than precision.

Game situations and decision points

Imagine this scenario.

You are approaching the final holes with a lead. Do you swing harder to finish strong, or do you protect position and let others make mistakes?

Financially, this mirrors retirement income planning. Protecting capital matters more than chasing returns.

Another scenario.

You are early in your career and tempted to delay saving because retirement feels far away. That is like skipping practice early in the season and expecting peak performance later.

Time is the advantage you cannot replace.

A third scenario.

You change jobs and must decide what to do with an old retirement account. Do you leave it behind, cash it out, or roll it forward intentionally?

Transitions create opportunity and risk. Awareness prevents regret.

Common athlete mistakes and financial parallels

One common mistake is underestimating longevity.

Athletes know careers can end suddenly, but life can last a long time. Planning must account for decades, not years.

Another mistake is viewing retirement accounts as inaccessible or irrelevant. They are tools, not cages. Used correctly, they create freedom.

A third mistake is waiting for clarity before starting. Clarity comes from action, not delay.

Golfers improve by playing, not by planning to play.

Winning the long game

Retirement accounts are not about retirement.

They are about independence.

They allow you to choose how you spend time later in life. They reduce pressure. They create options. They turn effort today into freedom tomorrow.

Great golfers think beyond the current hole.

Great financial plans think beyond the current paycheck.

When you use employer plans effectively, balance traditional and Roth accounts, respect contribution rules, and plan for income thoughtfully, financial independence becomes achievable.

That is not an ending.

It is the next chapter of the game.

Athlete Takeaways

- Independence is the goal, not a date on the calendar
- Employer plans and matches are part of your compensation
- Mixing tax-deferred and tax-free accounts creates options
- Retirement accounts work best when left alone to compound
- The long game rewards early reps and steady discipline

Chapter 21: Housing and Major Financial Decisions

Every golfer remembers the first time a single decision changed the entire round.

One aggressive line. One poor club choice. One rushed swing. Suddenly every hole after feels harder. The scorecard does not lie. Big decisions shape everything that follows.

Housing and other major financial choices work the same way.

These decisions do not show up every day, but when they do, they matter a lot. Where you live. How you finance it. What you drive. How much flexibility you keep. These choices affect cash flow, stress, and long-term options far more than most investment tweaks ever will.

This chapter is about learning to treat major financial decisions with the same discipline you would give to a critical shot under pressure.

Renting vs buying

Renting and buying are not moral decisions.

One is not winning and the other losing. They are tools that fit different seasons of life. The mistake is assuming one is always better without considering context.

Renting provides flexibility.

You can move easily. Expenses are more predictable. Maintenance is not your responsibility. Renting often makes sense early in a career, during transitions, or when location flexibility matters. It allows you to focus on saving, investing, and building stability without tying up capital.

Buying provides stability and long-term ownership.

Mortgage payments build equity over time. Housing costs may become more predictable. Emotional benefits matter too. Feeling settled can have real value. But buying also introduces responsibility. Maintenance. Taxes. Insurance. Repairs. These costs are real and often underestimated.

In golf terms, renting is playing a course with generous landing areas. Buying is committing to a tighter layout with more responsibility but potentially better long-term positioning.

The right decision depends on time horizon.

If you expect to move in a few years, renting often makes sense. If you plan to stay put long term and have stable income, buying can be a strong fit. The mistake is letting outside pressure drive the decision.

Golfers choose tees based on their game, not their ego. Housing decisions deserve the same honesty.

Mortgages and down payments

A mortgage is leverage.

It allows you to control a large asset with a smaller upfront investment. Leverage can help when used carefully. It can also magnify mistakes when used poorly.

Down payments matter because they determine risk.

A larger down payment reduces monthly payments and provides cushion if values fluctuate. A smaller down payment preserves cash but increases leverage and risk. Neither choice is automatically right. The key is understanding tradeoffs.

Mortgage terms matter too.

Interest rate. Loan length. Fixed versus adjustable. These details affect long-term cost and cash flow. Choosing the lowest monthly payment without understanding total cost is a common mistake.

Golfers know this lesson well.

Choosing a club only because it feels easy often creates problems later in the hole. Smart players think two shots ahead. Mortgage decisions require the same thinking.

Being house-rich and cash-poor is a dangerous position.

Liquidity matters. Owning a home does not help if cash flow is strained and flexibility disappears. Balance matters more than maximizing purchase price.

Cars, leases, and financing traps

Cars are one of the fastest ways to sabotage financial progress.

They depreciate. They are marketed aggressively. Financing makes expensive choices feel manageable. Many athletes fall into traps here because payments look affordable relative to income.

Leasing can make sense in specific situations.

Lower monthly payments. Predictable costs. Frequent upgrades. The tradeoff is that you never build ownership. Leasing prioritizes convenience over long-term cost efficiency.

Buying and financing a car builds ownership, but loan terms matter.

Long loan terms reduce payments but increase total cost and trap you in depreciating assets longer. Rolling negative equity into new loans compounds mistakes quietly.

In golf terms, this is forcing shots because the lie looks playable.

It works until it does not. Then recovery becomes difficult.

Transportation should support your life, not define it. Choosing reliable, reasonably priced vehicles preserves cash flow and reduces stress. Status fades quickly. Payments do not.

Planning major purchases

Major purchases extend beyond housing and cars.

Education. Business investments. Weddings. Renovations. These events often arrive with emotion attached. Emotion clouds judgment.

Planning is the difference.

Great golfers plan shots before stepping into the ball. Financially, planning means understanding total cost, timing, and impact on cash flow and goals.

Ask simple questions.

Can I afford this without sacrificing savings. How does this affect flexibility. What happens if income changes. Is this decision aligned with long-term priorities.

Impulse purchases create regret. Planned purchases create confidence.

Saving in advance reduces reliance on debt. Matching purchase timing to financial readiness matters more than opportunity cost fears.

Golfers know patience wins tournaments. Financial patience wins flexibility.

Game situations and decision points

Imagine this scenario.

You are standing on a reachable par five. The green is guarded by water. You could go for it, or you could lay up to a comfortable yardage. The decision depends on position, not desire.

Buying at the top of your budget feels like going for the green every time. Sometimes it works. Often it brings unnecessary danger into play.

Another scenario.

You see teammates or friends upgrading homes and cars. Pressure builds. Do you follow, or do you stick to your plan?

Comparison creates forced shots. Forced shots create mistakes.

A third scenario.

You delay planning because the decision feels big. Meanwhile, opportunities pass or costs rise. Avoidance is also a decision.

Preparation removes fear.

Common athlete mistakes and financial parallels

One common mistake is equating affordability with readiness.

Just because you can make the payment does not mean the decision fits your plan. Golfers know that clearing a hazard does not guarantee a good next shot.

Another mistake is underestimating maintenance and ownership costs. Expenses do not end at purchase.

A third mistake is letting emotion override math. Emotion belongs in motivation, not in major financial decisions.

Athletes succeed when they separate feeling from execution.

Winning the long game

Housing and major purchases shape the rhythm of your financial life.

They affect how much you can save. How much risk you can take. How flexible you remain when life changes. These decisions deserve respect.

Great golfers choose shots that keep the round manageable.

Great financial decisions keep life manageable.

You do not need perfect choices. You need thoughtful ones. Decisions aligned with goals. Choices that preserve flexibility. Purchases that support your life instead of controlling it.

When major financial decisions are made intentionally, everything else becomes easier to manage.

That is how you stay in position for the long season.

Athlete Takeaways

- Big decisions shape the entire round
- Renting and buying are tools for different seasons
- Leverage helps only when risk is understood
- Payments that feel easy can hide long-term damage
- Planning purchases protects flexibility and confidence

Chapter 22: Your Career Is Your Longest Round

Every golfer eventually realizes one round does not define a career. You can play great today and struggle tomorrow. You can start slow and finish strong. What matters is showing up year after year, making adjustments, and staying healthy enough to compete. Careers work the same way. One paycheck does not define financial success. One job does not determine your future.

Your career is your longest round.

It is the primary engine that fuels every other financial decision. Investing, saving, housing, and lifestyle all depend on how income is earned and managed over time. Understanding your career the way a golfer understands a season changes how you approach money.

Salary vs total compensation

Many people focus only on salary.

Salary is visible. It is easy to compare. It feels like the scoreboard. But total compensation tells the real story. Benefits, bonuses, retirement contributions, health insurance, equity, and flexibility all matter.

Two jobs with the same salary can produce very different financial outcomes.

Employer retirement matches add long-term value. Health benefits reduce risk. Paid time off supports balance. Equity or profit sharing can create upside. Ignoring these factors is like judging a round by one hole.

Golfers know better.

You do not evaluate performance based on one shot. You look at the entire card. Total compensation is the full scorecard of a job offer.

Understanding total compensation allows better decisions. It prevents chasing headline numbers while missing quiet value.

Job changes and benefits

Career changes are normal.

Athletes change teams. Coaches change roles. Careers evolve. Each transition creates opportunity and risk. Understanding benefits during transitions prevents costly mistakes.

When changing jobs, benefits often reset.

Health coverage changes. Retirement plans change. Vesting schedules may be affected. Overlooking these details can create gaps. Gaps create stress.

Golfers prepare for new courses.

They study layouts. Yardages. Hazards. Financially, preparing for a new job requires the same attention. Understanding how benefits change keeps momentum intact.

Rollovers matter.

Old retirement accounts should be handled intentionally. Leaving them behind, cashing them out, or rolling them forward all have consequences. Awareness prevents regret.

Negotiation basics

Negotiation is not confrontation.

It is communication. It is clarity. It is advocating for value respectfully. Athletes negotiate roles, scholarships, playing time, and contracts. Financial negotiation works the same way.

Preparation matters.

Know your value. Understand market ranges. Be clear about priorities.

Salary. Benefits. Flexibility. Growth. Negotiation is about alignment, not winning.

Timing matters too.

Negotiating at the right moment increases success. Demanding without context creates friction. Golfers know this. You do not force shots at the wrong time.

Many people avoid negotiation out of discomfort. That avoidance has long-term cost. Small differences compounded over a career become significant.

Confidence grows with practice.

Negotiation is a skill. Like any skill, it improves with reps.

Side income and entrepreneurship

Side income adds flexibility.

It diversifies income sources. It reduces dependence on a single employer. For athletes especially, side income can extend identity and create opportunities beyond competition.

Entrepreneurship requires discipline.

Side projects demand time, energy, and patience. Not every idea works. Not every opportunity fits. The mistake is chasing everything instead of building intentionally.

In golf terms, side income is like practicing different shot shapes.

It expands capability. It increases adaptability. But it should not disrupt fundamentals.

Side income also brings responsibility.

Taxes. Recordkeeping. Cash flow management. Ignoring these details creates problems. Understanding them creates opportunity.

Not every athlete needs a side business. But everyone benefits from understanding how income diversification affects flexibility and risk.

Game situations and decision points

Imagine this scenario.

You are midway through a long season. You feel undervalued. Do you quit impulsively, or do you prepare, assess options, and move strategically?

Career decisions deserve the same discipline as critical shots.

Another scenario.

You receive a higher salary offer with weaker benefits. Do you chase the headline number, or do you evaluate total compensation?

The scoreboard does not tell the full story.

A third scenario.

You are offered a side opportunity that sounds exciting but strains time and focus. Do you take it without planning, or do you evaluate fit?

Opportunity cost matters.

Common athlete mistakes and financial parallels

One common mistake is equating effort with value. Hard work matters, but positioning matters too.

Another mistake is avoiding uncomfortable conversations. Avoidance delays growth.

A third mistake is underestimating burnout. Longevity requires balance.

Athletes who succeed long term think strategically about seasons, not just games.

Winning the long game

Your career fuels everything else.

Treating it like a long round creates perspective. You stop overreacting to short-term setbacks. You plan transitions. You negotiate thoughtfully. You build optionality.

Golfers who last understand pacing.

They train. They recover. They adapt. Financially, managing your career with intention creates stability, growth, and freedom.

Income earned wisely supports investing. Investing supports independence. Independence supports choice.

That is how long careers and strong financial lives are built.

Athlete Takeaways

- Your career fuels every other financial decision
- Salary is only part of the scorecard
- Preparation makes negotiation easier
- Side income adds flexibility when built intentionally
- Think in seasons, not just paychecks

Chapter 23: Estate Planning Basics Everyone Needs

Every golfer eventually plays a round they will not finish.

Weather rolls in. Darkness falls. Injury happens. The round ends earlier than planned. The smart players think about this before it happens. They know what to do. Who takes over. Where equipment goes. Nothing is left to guesswork.

Estate planning exists for the same reason.

It is not about expecting something bad to happen. It is about being responsible for the people and resources connected to you. Estate planning is a plan for incapacity, death, and transition. It ensures that decisions are made by people you trust and that assets move according to your wishes, not default rules.

This chapter is about understanding the basic documents everyone needs and why waiting creates unnecessary problems.

Wills and trusts

A will is the foundation.

It states who receives your assets, who manages the process, and who cares for minor children if applicable. Without a will, state law decides. Those default rules rarely match personal intent.

A trust is a structure.

It holds assets and provides instructions for how and when they are distributed. Trusts can reduce delays, provide privacy, and add control. They are especially useful when beneficiaries are minors, have special needs, or when complexity exists.

Wills and trusts are not competing tools.

They work together. The right structure depends on your situation, assets, and goals. The mistake is assuming estate planning is only for the wealthy. Responsibility is not about net worth. It is about clarity.

Golfers understand preparation.

You do not wait until conditions are bad to plan. Estate planning is preparation, not prediction.

Beneficiaries and account titling

Many assets pass outside of a will.

Retirement accounts. Insurance policies. Bank accounts. These assets transfer based on beneficiary designations and titling, not on what a will says. This is one of the most common and costly misunderstandings.

Beneficiary designations must be accurate and updated.

Life changes. Marriage. Divorce. Children. Death. Outdated designations cause unintended outcomes. Fixing them is usually simple. Ignoring them is expensive.

Account titling matters too.

Joint ownership, transfer-on-death designations, and trust ownership affect how assets move. Understanding how accounts are titled prevents delays and disputes.

In golf terms, this is knowing which rules apply to which areas of the course.

You cannot play by assumptions. You play by the rules that govern that situation. Estate planning works the same way.

Powers of attorney

Incapacity planning is often overlooked.

A power of attorney allows someone you trust to make financial decisions on your behalf if you cannot. Without it, families may need court involvement to manage basic tasks. That process is slow, public, and stressful.

There are different types.

A general power of attorney covers broad financial matters. A durable power of attorney remains effective if you become incapacitated. Choosing the right person matters more than choosing the document.

This role requires trust.

The person named should be responsible, available, and aligned with your values. Avoiding this decision does not remove the need. It removes control.

Golfers designate captains for a reason. Leadership matters when pressure shows up.

Healthcare directives

Healthcare decisions deserve clarity.

A healthcare directive outlines your wishes for medical treatment if you cannot communicate. It may include a living will and a healthcare proxy who can make decisions on your behalf.

These documents reduce conflict.

They guide family members during stressful moments. They ensure your values are respected. They prevent guessing and disagreement.

Many people avoid this topic because it feels uncomfortable. Avoidance shifts burden onto loved ones. Clarity is a gift.

Golfers communicate strategy clearly. Confusion during execution leads to mistakes. Healthcare planning prevents that confusion.

Game situations and decision points

Imagine this scenario.

You are sidelined unexpectedly. Decisions need to be made quickly. Do your loved ones know your wishes, or are they guessing under pressure?

Estate planning answers that question before it is asked.

Another scenario.

You assume everything will pass through your will. Later, beneficiaries are outdated and assets go somewhere unintended. That is like playing by the wrong rules and being shocked by the result.

A third scenario.

Life changes, but documents do not. Reviews prevent misalignment.

Common athlete mistakes and financial parallels

One common mistake is thinking estate planning can wait. Delaying creates exposure.

Another mistake is assuming simple equals sufficient. Simplicity is good, but clarity is essential.

A third mistake is avoiding conversations. Silence creates confusion.

Athletes who lead communicate early and clearly.

Winning the long game

Estate planning is not about control from beyond.

It is about care.

It protects loved ones. It reduces stress. It ensures that your work, discipline, and resources continue to serve the people and causes you care about.

Great golfers plan for contingencies.

Great financial plans do the same.

When wills, trusts, beneficiaries, powers of attorney, and healthcare directives are in place, uncertainty shrinks. Confidence grows. Loved ones are protected.

That is not morbid.

That is responsible.

Athlete Takeaways

- Planning removes pressure when it matters most
- Wills and trusts provide clarity and control
- Beneficiaries override assumptions every time
- Powers of attorney protect against uncertainty
- Clear healthcare wishes are a gift to others

Chapter 24: Talking About Money With Family

Every golfer has learned this lesson.

Silence creates mistakes.

If expectations are not clear, shots get misplayed. If roles are not defined, confusion shows up under pressure. Teams that communicate well make fewer errors. Teams that avoid hard conversations pay for it later.

Money works the same way in families.

Most financial stress inside families does not come from lack of income. It comes from lack of communication. Assumptions. Avoidance. Unspoken expectations. Talking about money feels uncomfortable for many people, but avoiding the conversation does not protect relationships. It strains them.

This chapter is about learning how to talk about money with family in a way that builds understanding instead of conflict.

Teaching kids about money

Money habits are formed early.

Kids are always watching. How money is talked about. How decisions are made. How stress shows up. Silence teaches just as much as instruction. If money is never discussed, kids fill the gap with assumptions.

Teaching kids about money does not require complex lessons.

It starts with basics. What money is. How it is earned. Why choices matter. Allowances, chores, saving jars, and simple budgets teach cause and effect.

Kids learn that money represents effort and tradeoffs.

Consistency matters more than perfection.

Golfers know this well. Reps build skill. Occasional lectures do not. Small, repeated conversations build understanding over time.

As kids get older, responsibility should grow.

Teenagers can learn about bank accounts, debit cards, and budgeting. Mistakes made with small amounts teach valuable lessons without serious consequences. Shielding kids completely delays learning and increases risk later.

The goal is not to raise financial experts.

The goal is to raise adults who are comfortable making decisions, asking questions, and understanding consequences.

College and young adults

College and early adulthood are critical transition periods.

Income may be limited. Freedom increases. Decisions multiply. Many young adults are making financial choices for the first time without guidance. Credit cards. Student loans. Housing. These decisions shape years of outcomes.

Parents often struggle with where to step in and where to step back.

Support without clarity creates dependency. No support creates fear. The balance is communication.

Conversations should focus on expectations.

Who pays for what. What support exists. What boundaries matter. Clear expectations reduce resentment on both sides. Silence creates mismatched assumptions.

Young adults also need space to learn.

Mistakes will happen. Golfers know development includes bad rounds. Financial growth requires similar patience. The role of family is guidance, not control.

Open conversations normalize questions.

When money is discussed openly, young adults are more likely to ask before making mistakes instead of hiding them afterward.

Aging parents and caregiving

Money conversations shift again as parents age.

Health changes. Income may become fixed. Care needs increase. Avoiding these conversations does not delay reality. It delays preparation.

Caregiving decisions involve finances.

Who pays for what. How care is funded. What resources exist. These topics are emotionally charged because they involve roles reversing. That discomfort makes avoidance tempting.

Preparation reduces stress.

Understanding parents' wishes, financial situation, and planning documents prevents crisis decisions later. These conversations are not about control. They are about respect.

Golfers prepare for changing conditions.

They adjust strategy as daylight fades or weather changes. Financial planning for aging parents is the same kind of adjustment. Early conversations preserve dignity and choice.

Family alignment matters.

When siblings are involved, transparency prevents conflict. Unspoken expectations create resentment. Clear communication creates shared responsibility.

Family expectations and boundaries

Boundaries are essential.

Without them, money becomes a source of tension. Loans without clarity. Support without limits. Expectations without agreement. These situations damage relationships.

Setting boundaries is not selfish.

It is responsible. Boundaries protect relationships by preventing misunderstandings. They allow generosity to be intentional instead of resentful.

Clear boundaries include clarity on support.

What you can help with. What you cannot. Under what conditions. These conversations feel awkward initially. They prevent years of tension later.

Golfers understand boundaries instinctively.

You play within course limits for a reason. Ignoring boundaries leads to penalties. Financial boundaries work the same way.

Boundaries also go both directions.

Parents need boundaries with adult children. Adult children need boundaries with parents. Extended family needs clarity. No one benefits from silent expectations.

Game situations and decision points

Imagine this situation.

A teammate assumes you will cover something financially because you never said otherwise. You feel pressure but resentment builds. That is a communication failure, not a money problem.

Another scenario.

A child makes a financial mistake but is afraid to talk about it because money has always been a tense topic. Silence compounds damage.

Another scenario.

A family waits until a health crisis to discuss caregiving and finances. Decisions are rushed. Emotions run high. Preparation would have changed everything.

Golfers plan ahead to avoid scrambling under pressure. Families need the same discipline.

Common athlete mistakes and financial parallels

One common mistake is avoiding conversations to keep peace. Temporary peace often leads to long-term conflict.

Another mistake is assuming shared values without discussion. Assumptions break under stress.

A third mistake is letting guilt drive decisions. Guilt-based money choices rarely age well.

Athletes know that honest feedback improves performance. Families improve through honest communication too.

Winning the long game

Talking about money with family is not about having all the answers.

It is about openness. Listening. Clarity. Respect. These conversations evolve as life changes. They are not one-time events. They are ongoing check-ins.

Great golfers communicate constantly.

They talk strategy. They adjust roles. They reset expectations. Financial communication works the same way.

When money is discussed openly, kids learn confidence instead of fear. Young adults learn responsibility instead of secrecy. Aging parents experience dignity instead of crisis. Families strengthen instead of fracture.

Money will always exist.

How you talk about it determines whether it brings people together or pushes them apart.

Athlete Takeaways

- Silence creates mistakes under pressure
- Early reps build lifelong money confidence
- Clear expectations reduce resentment
- Boundaries protect relationships, not wallets
- Communication is part of long-term success

Part VI: Winning the Match Over Time

Every golfer who has played competitive matches understands one truth.

Winning is rarely about a single hole.

Matches are won over time. Through patience. Through resilience. Through making fewer mistakes than the person across from you. Momentum shifts. Pressure builds. Conditions change. The player who wins is usually the one who stays disciplined the longest, not the one who flashes brilliance early.

Financial success works the same way.

This final section of the book is about perspective. It is about understanding that money is not a sprint, a hot streak, or a lucky break. It is a match played over decades. The decisions you make repeatedly matter far more than the decisions you make once.

Up to this point, the book has focused on fundamentals, protection, investing, execution, and life context. All of those pieces matter. But none of them work if you cannot sustain them over time. Winning the financial match requires habits that hold up through change.

One of the biggest mistakes people make with money is assuming the hardest part is learning what to do.

It is not.

The hardest part is continuing to do the right things when boredom, fear, confidence, or fatigue show up. Golfers know this feeling well. The basics never change, but motivation fluctuates. Energy dips. Doubt creeps in. The match tests your ability to stay committed long after the excitement fades.

Long-term success favors people who simplify.

Simple systems. Clear rules. Repeatable habits. Over time, complexity creates friction. Friction leads to avoidance. Avoidance leads to mistakes. Simplicity keeps the game playable.

This section also emphasizes awareness.

Life will change. Careers shift. Families grow. Health evolves. Markets move. A good plan adapts without losing its core. Winning the match does not mean refusing to adjust. It means adjusting without abandoning discipline.

Golfers do this instinctively.

They change strategy based on match play dynamics. They protect leads. They press when opportunity appears. They stay patient when conditions are difficult. Financial maturity looks the same.

Another key theme here is humility.

No one plays a perfect financial match. Mistakes happen. Opportunities are missed. Outcomes differ from expectations. The difference between long-term success and long-term stress is how you respond to those moments.

Do you panic and overcorrect, or do you reset and refocus.

Do you let one bad hole define the match, or do you trust that steady play still wins.

Money rewards humility because it punishes certainty. Markets do not care how confident you feel. Life does not follow scripts. Planning exists to create resilience, not control.

Winning the match over time also means knowing when to ask for help.

Even the best golfers rely on coaches. Caddies. Advisors. Feedback matters. Financial decisions become more complex as assets grow and responsibilities increase. Seeking guidance is not weakness. It is strategy.

This section will focus on recognizing bad advice, understanding when professional help adds value, and identifying behaviors that quietly undermine long-term success. These topics matter because mistakes compound. Good habits compound too.

The final idea is legacy.

Winning financially is not just about personal outcomes. It is about what remains. The example you set. The stability you create. The freedom you pass on. Athletes understand legacy deeply. Records fade. Impact lasts.

Money is a tool. Used well, it supports independence, generosity, and peace of mind. Used poorly, it creates stress and regret. The difference is not intelligence. It is discipline over time.

Winning the financial match does not require perfection.

It requires patience.

It requires structure.

It requires the willingness to keep playing smart golf even when no one is watching.

That is how matches are won.

Chapter 25: Advisors, Scams, and Long-Term Success

Every golfer eventually reaches a point where self-coaching is not enough.

You can grind on the range. You can watch film. You can read books. But at some stage, progress slows without outside perspective. Blind spots develop. Bad habits sneak in. The players who last and win over time are the ones who know when to bring in help and who to trust when they do.

Money works the same way.

Long-term financial success is not about knowing everything. It is about avoiding big mistakes, filtering noise, and building habits that hold up for decades. This final chapter is about knowing when to seek help, how to recognize good guidance versus bad advice, and what actually determines success over time.

When to seek professional help

Needing help is not failure.

It is strategy.

In golf, you bring in a coach when stakes rise or when complexity increases. Financially, professional help becomes valuable when decisions affect multiple areas at once. Taxes, investments, insurance, estate planning, business decisions. When one move impacts many others, coordination matters.

Common moments when help makes sense include career transitions, sudden income changes, selling a business, receiving an inheritance, getting married, having children, or approaching retirement. These moments introduce complexity and consequences.

Another reason to seek help is emotional.

If money decisions create stress, anxiety, or avoidance, structure and guidance can restore confidence. A good advisor does not just give answers. They provide perspective and accountability.

The mistake is waiting until something goes wrong.

Golfers do not wait until their swing collapses mid-season to seek instruction. Financial guidance works best when it is proactive, not reactive.

Types of financial advisors

Not all advisors are the same.

Understanding roles prevents disappointment.

Some advisors focus primarily on investments. Others specialize in comprehensive financial planning. Some are paid through fees. Others earn commissions. How someone is paid influences incentives. Transparency matters.

A true planning relationship looks at the entire picture.

Cash flow. Goals. Risk. Taxes. Protection. Investments. Estate considerations. Career decisions. The value is not in stock picks. It is in coordination.

In golf terms, this is the difference between a swing coach and a full performance team. Both can help, but the scope matters.

The most important factor is alignment.

An advisor should listen more than they talk. They should explain clearly. They should help you understand tradeoffs instead of promising certainty. If pressure replaces education, that is a warning sign.

Trust is built through clarity, not confidence.

Recognizing scams and bad advice

Scams target emotion.

Urgency. Exclusivity. Fear. Greed. Promises of guaranteed returns. Pressure to act quickly. These tactics bypass logic and push people into decisions they do not fully understand.

If something sounds too good to be true, it usually is.

No legitimate investment guarantees high returns without risk. No honest advisor discourages questions. No sound strategy requires secrecy.

Bad advice is not always a scam.

Sometimes it is well-meaning but misaligned. Advice that ignores your goals, timeline, or risk tolerance can still cause damage. Copying someone else's strategy without context is one of the most common mistakes athletes make.

Golfers know this lesson well.

Just because a swing works for one player does not mean it works for another. Financial advice works the same way.

Ten common financial mistakes

1. Chasing quick wins instead of building consistency
2. Ignoring fundamentals while focusing on advanced strategies
3. Taking on more lifestyle than cash flow supports
4. Confusing volatility with failure
5. Letting emotion drive decisions
6. Overconfidence after short-term success
7. Avoiding uncomfortable topics like taxes or estate planning
8. Waiting too long to start
9. Copying others without understanding context
10. Believing activity equals progress

These mistakes are not about intelligence. They are about behavior. Awareness reduces their power.

Ten rules for long-term success

1. Master fundamentals before chasing complexity
2. Spend less than you earn consistently
3. Build protection before taking risk
4. Invest with a long-term mindset
5. Diversify intentionally
6. Automate good behavior
7. Ignore noise and comparison
8. Review periodically, not constantly
9. Adjust without panic
10. Stay disciplined longer than others

These rules are simple on purpose. Simple rules are easier to follow under pressure.

Winning the long game

Long-term financial success is not about being perfect.

It is about staying in the game.

Avoiding scams. Recognizing bad advice. Seeking help when appropriate. Building habits that work quietly over time. These behaviors compound just like returns do.

Great golfers win matches by being steady.

They do not need to dominate every hole. They need to avoid big mistakes, trust their preparation, and stay patient when momentum shifts.

Money rewards the same approach.

If you master fundamentals, protect yourself from obvious risks, invest with discipline, and keep perspective, you give yourself a strong chance to win the match over time.

The goal is not to beat everyone else.

Chapter 26: Losing the Schedule and Rebuilding Structure

Every athlete remembers the moment structure disappears.

No more mandatory workouts. No more lift times posted on the wall. No more film sessions you did not choose. No coach checking attendance. No strength staff tracking reps. One day, your calendar goes from being completely full to completely empty.

At first, that freedom feels incredible.

Then life quietly gets harder.

This chapter is about what happens when external structure disappears and how rebuilding personal structure is one of the most important financial and life skills former athletes must develop. The loss of a schedule does not just affect fitness. It affects money, habits, discipline, and long-term stability.

Why life gets harder when no one is setting your calendar

Athletes are trained inside systems.

Your day is planned for you. When to wake up. When to train. When to eat. When to recover. That structure creates rhythm. Rhythm creates consistency. Consistency creates performance.

When that structure is removed, many athletes assume discipline alone will replace it.

It rarely does.

Without a calendar setting expectations, decisions multiply. When to work out. When to eat. When to work. When to rest. When to spend. When to save. Decision fatigue sets in. Good intentions slowly get replaced by convenience.

Golfers understand this immediately.

You can have a great swing, but without a routine, performance becomes inconsistent. Financial habits work the same way. Structure matters more than motivation.

The absence of structure does not cause failure overnight. It causes drift. Drift is dangerous because it feels harmless while it compounds.

From mandatory workouts to optional discipline

In sports, discipline is enforced.

You show up or you sit. You lift or you run. The consequences are immediate and visible. In life after sports, discipline becomes optional. There is no whistle. No depth chart. No penalty for skipping today.

Optional discipline is harder than mandatory discipline.

Financial habits suffer first. Automatic saving stops. Spending creeps up. Bills get paid late. Investing becomes reactive instead of planned. Nothing feels urgent until something breaks.

Athletes often blame themselves for this shift.

They assume they lost discipline. The truth is they lost structure. Discipline without structure is fragile. Structure without motivation still works.

Golfers know this lesson.

You do not rely on feel alone. You rely on routine. Setup. Pre-shot habits. Those systems protect performance when confidence dips. Financial systems do the same thing.

How lack of structure quietly breaks financial habits

The damage is subtle.

Savings become irregular. Investing gets delayed. Expenses grow because there is no framework to push against them. Lifestyle expands to fill available space. Without guardrails, money flows wherever attention goes.

This is not reckless behavior.

It is unstructured behavior.

When paychecks arrive without a plan, spending decisions become emotional. When saving is not scheduled, it gets postponed. When investing is not automated, it gets timed poorly.

Structure creates default behavior.

In sports, default behavior is showing up. In money, default behavior should be saving, investing, and protecting progress. Without systems, default behavior becomes consumption.

Golfers see this when rounds fall apart late.

Fatigue shows up. Focus fades. The swing did not change. The structure supporting execution did.

Replacing practice schedules with personal systems

The solution is not willpower.

The solution is rebuilding structure intentionally.

Personal systems replace team schedules. Calendars replace coaches. Automation replaces accountability partners. The goal is not to recreate sports life. The goal is to recreate consistency.

Start with fixed anchors.

Wake-up times. Workout blocks. Work blocks. Meal planning. Review times. These anchors reduce decisions. Fewer decisions protect discipline.

Financial anchors matter too.

Paydays trigger automatic transfers. Savings moves first. Investing happens on schedule. Bills are paid automatically. Reviews happen quarterly, not daily.

Golfers use routines to remove doubt.

You stand over the ball already committed. Financial routines do the same thing. They remove emotion from execution.

Structure also creates identity.

When you know who you are supposed to be each day, behavior follows. Without structure, identity becomes fluid. Fluid identity leads to inconsistent habits.

Athletes thrive with defined roles.

Post-sport life requires self-defined roles. Builder. Saver. Investor. Parent. Professional. Structure reinforces those roles.

Game situations and decision points

Imagine this situation.

You wake up with no obligations. No schedule. No deadlines. Do you drift through the day reacting, or do you execute a plan you already decided on?

Financially, this is the difference between reacting to expenses and executing a cash flow plan.

Another scenario.

You miss a workout or a savings transfer. Do you abandon the system or reset and continue?

Golfers know one bad hole does not end the round. Structure allows recovery without shame.

A third scenario.

Your income increases, but your systems stay the same. Do you let lifestyle creep take over, or do you update structure to capture progress?

Structure must evolve as life changes.

Common athlete mistakes and financial parallels

One mistake is assuming freedom means flexibility.

Freedom without structure becomes chaos. Golfers do not play their best golf without routines. Money behaves the same way.

Another mistake is waiting for motivation.

Motivation is unreliable. Systems are not. Champions train when motivation is low because structure exists.

A third mistake is copying others.

Your structure must fit your life. Borrowing someone else's schedule rarely works. Golfers know that swing copying without fit creates problems.

Winning the long game

Life after sports rewards self-leadership.

No one is coming to build your schedule. No one is enforcing discipline. No one is protecting your financial habits except you and the systems you create.

This is not a disadvantage.

It is an opportunity.

When structure is rebuilt intentionally, life becomes calmer. Financial progress becomes automatic. Stress decreases. Confidence returns.

Great golfers are self-sufficient.

They own their routines. They trust their systems. They adjust when needed without abandoning fundamentals.

Financial success after sports works the same way.

Rebuild structure. Automate discipline. Protect habits. Let systems carry you when motivation fades.

That is how consistency survives without a coach.

That is how the long game is won.

Athlete Takeaways

- Discipline fades without structure, systems do not
- Optional habits break faster than scheduled ones
- Automation replaces accountability when no one is watching
- Routines protect performance when motivation dips
- Structure is how freedom actually works

Chapter 27: From Teammates to Coworkers

Every former athlete remembers the first day in a non-sports workplace.

You show up on time. You are prepared. You are ready to work. And yet, something feels off. There is no locker room. No shared warm-up. No clear captain. No scoreboard. People sit at desks, talk in meetings, and send emails that feel vague compared to the direct language you are used to.

The transition from teammates to coworkers is one of the most underestimated challenges athletes face after sports. It is not about work ethic. Athletes usually have that covered. It is about environment, expectations, and how performance is evaluated. This shift has a direct impact on income growth, job satisfaction, and long-term career stability.

Why the workplace feels foreign after sports

Sports environments are built on clarity.

You know the goal. Win the game. You know the standard. Compete every rep. You know your role. Starter, backup, specialist. You know how success is measured. Film does not lie. The scoreboard settles debates.

Most workplaces are the opposite.

Goals are often abstract. Expectations change. Success is subjective. Performance reviews happen infrequently and may not reflect daily effort. This mismatch creates frustration for athletes who are used to clear rules and immediate feedback.

Athletes are conditioned to operate in high-accountability systems. When that structure disappears, confusion replaces confidence. That confusion can lead to underperformance, not because ability dropped, but because the rules of the game changed.

Golfers feel this too when moving from tournament play to casual rounds. The intensity drops. Feedback disappears. Focus becomes optional. Performance suffers unless structure is recreated intentionally.

Authority without coaches

In sports, authority is obvious.

Head coach. Position coach. Strength coach. Their roles are defined. Their authority is clear. Instructions are direct. Disagreements are settled quickly. You may not always like the decision, but you understand who makes it.

Workplaces rarely function this way.

Authority is layered. Managers may not be experts. Decision-makers may be distant. Influence often matters more than title. This can feel unsettling for athletes used to direct leadership.

Athletes often assume that effort alone earns trust and advancement. In sports, that is often true. In workplaces, effort must be paired with communication and visibility. Hard work that is not understood or recognized does not always translate into opportunity.

Learning how authority works in a workplace is part of career development.

Who actually makes decisions. How priorities are set. What metrics matter. These answers are rarely written down. Athletes who fail to learn this landscape often stall despite strong performance.

Feedback without film

Athletes are built on feedback.

Film sessions. Practice reps. Game stats. Corrections are specific and immediate. You know exactly what you did wrong and how to fix it.

In most jobs, feedback is sparse.

You might hear nothing for months. Silence is often interpreted as approval, but that assumption can be dangerous. Performance reviews may focus on vague themes rather than concrete actions.

This lack of feedback creates anxiety.

Athletes start guessing. Am I doing well. Am I valued. Should I push harder or pull back. Guessing leads to inconsistency.

The solution is proactive feedback.

Former athletes must learn to ask for clarity. What does success look like in this role. How is performance evaluated. What would improvement look like over the next six months. These questions feel unnecessary in sports. In the workplace, they are essential.

Golfers check yardages and green speeds before swinging. Career development requires the same information gathering.

Politics, ambiguity, and unclear expectations

This is often the hardest adjustment.

Sports are political in their own way, but outcomes are still performance-driven. Play well and you play. Perform poorly and you sit. While not perfect, the link between effort and outcome is usually visible.

Workplace politics are less direct.

Relationships matter. Perception matters. Timing matters. Decisions may be influenced by factors unrelated to performance. This can feel unfair to athletes who believe the work should speak for itself.

Ambiguity increases risk.

Unclear expectations lead to misaligned effort. You may be optimizing for the wrong outcomes. That misalignment slows income growth and limits advancement.

Understanding workplace culture is part of the job.

What behaviors are rewarded. How communication happens. How conflict is handled. These dynamics affect stability and earnings just as much as technical skill.

Ignoring them does not make them go away. It just makes outcomes less predictable.

How this impacts income growth and career stability

Career progression in most fields is not automatic.

Raises, promotions, and opportunities depend on a mix of performance, perception, and positioning. Athletes who rely solely on effort may find themselves overlooked.

This is not a criticism of athletes. It is a reality of different systems.

Income growth requires strategic awareness.

You need to understand how value is created in your organization. What problems generate revenue. What skills are scarce. What results are visible to decision-makers. Aligning your effort with those factors increases stability and earnings.

Career stability also depends on adaptability.

Roles change. Companies change. Markets change. Athletes who treat careers like long seasons, adjusting strategy as conditions change, tend to last longer and earn more.

Golfers do not play every course the same way. Careers should not be managed rigidly either.

Game situations and decision points

Imagine this scenario.

You are working hard, but recognition is minimal. Do you assume effort will eventually be noticed, or do you seek clarity and adjust how your work is communicated?

Another scenario.

You receive vague feedback like "doing fine." Do you accept it, or do you ask what "great" would look like?

A third scenario.

Office politics frustrate you. Do you disengage, or do you learn how influence actually works in that environment?

These decisions compound over time.

Common athlete mistakes and career parallels

One common mistake is assuming fairness is automatic.

Sports condition athletes to expect merit-based outcomes. Workplaces are more complex.

Another mistake is avoiding feedback.

Silence feels safer than potential criticism. Lack of clarity creates more risk than honest conversation.

A third mistake is equating discomfort with failure.

Feeling out of place does not mean you are doing poorly. It means you are learning a new game.

Athletes who succeed post-sports treat this transition as skill development, not identity loss.

Winning the long game

Moving from teammates to coworkers requires a mindset shift.

You are still competing, but the rules are different. Performance matters, but communication and context matter too. Structure is less visible, so you must create your own.

Former athletes who thrive learn the new game deliberately.

They seek clarity. They ask questions. They understand incentives. They adapt without losing their work ethic.

Golfers who travel and play new courses prepare differently each time. Careers demand the same respect.

When you learn how workplaces actually function, confusion fades. Confidence returns. Income growth becomes intentional. Stability improves.

This is not about lowering standards.

It is about translating elite habits into a new environment.

Athlete Takeaways

- New games require learning new rules
- Effort matters, but clarity and visibility matter too
- Feedback does not come automatically, ask for it
- Understanding incentives drives income growth
- Adaptation is how long careers are built

Chapter 28: When No One Is Watching Anymore

Every athlete eventually faces the quietest moment of their life.

No crowd. No teammates looking over. No coach with a whistle. No scoreboard updating in real time. The work still needs to be done, but no one is watching to make sure it happens.

That moment reveals everything.

In sports, accountability is external. Attendance is taken. Film is reviewed. Effort is visible. Consequences are immediate. When that structure disappears, many former athletes discover a gap they did not know existed. Not a gap in ability. A gap in discipline when pressure is gone.

This chapter is about that discipline gap and why money mistakes often begin years before they show up on a statement.

The discipline gap after accountability disappears

Athletes are trained in public accountability.

You lift because someone is checking. You study film because it will be addressed. You show up because absence has consequences. That environment produces consistency even on days motivation is low.

Life after sports removes that framework.

No one checks if you saved this month. No one benches you for skipping retirement contributions. No one reviews your spending decisions on film. Without accountability, habits either become self-driven or slowly erode.

This gap surprises many former athletes.

They assume discipline is a personality trait. In reality, discipline is often environmental. When the environment changes, behavior changes unless new systems replace the old ones.

Golfers understand this perfectly.

Pre-shot routines exist because feel is unreliable. Routines protect execution when pressure or distraction shows up. Financial routines serve the same purpose when accountability fades.

Why former athletes self-sabotage without pressure

Self-sabotage rarely looks dramatic.

It looks like skipping one savings transfer. Delaying one investment decision. Letting expenses creep a little higher. Choosing convenience repeatedly over intention. None of these feel dangerous in isolation.

Over time, they compound.

Former athletes are especially vulnerable because they are used to pressure producing performance. When pressure disappears, urgency disappears too. Without urgency, habits soften.

This is not laziness.

It is a mismatch between training and environment. Athletes are trained to respond. Life after sports requires initiation. That shift is uncomfortable and often avoided.

Money exposes this quickly.

There is no adrenaline in budgeting. No crowd energy in long-term investing. No immediate feedback in saving consistently. Without systems, former athletes drift toward what feels good now instead of what matters later.

Comfort vs growth decisions

When no one is watching, comfort becomes tempting.

Sleep in. Spend freely. Avoid difficult conversations. Delay planning. Comfort is not evil. It just becomes dangerous when it replaces growth repeatedly.

In sports, comfort is the enemy.

You train when it hurts because improvement lives there. After sports, that same discomfort shows up differently. Saving instead of spending. Investing instead of waiting. Planning instead of avoiding. These choices are quiet and uncomfortable because they lack immediate reward.

Growth decisions feel boring.

Comfort decisions feel deserved.

Golfers know this tradeoff intimately.

Laying up feels boring. Going for the green feels exciting. Over a season, boring wins. Financially, boring decisions create stability. Exciting decisions often create regret.

When no one is watching, growth requires identity.

You must decide who you are when external validation disappears. Are you still someone who shows up. Someone who prepares. Someone who sacrifices short-term comfort for long-term success.

Money tests that identity relentlessly.

Translating grind culture into adult life

Grind culture works in sports because the system supports it.

Schedules exist. Recovery is planned. Purpose is clear. Adult life does not come with those supports. Grinding without structure leads to burnout, not progress.

Former athletes often try to replicate intensity without infrastructure.

They work harder without planning. Hustle without direction. Say yes to everything. Financially, this looks like earning well but saving poorly. Being busy but unprotected. Moving fast without clarity.

The grind needs translation.

In adult life, grind becomes consistency. It becomes systems. It becomes pacing. It becomes saying no strategically.

Golfers know this transition well.

You cannot play every round at tournament intensity. Longevity requires pacing. Financial success requires the same maturity.

True grind culture in adult life looks like boring excellence.

Automatic savings. Regular investing. Quarterly reviews. Clear boundaries. These are not exciting. They are effective.

Why money mistakes show up years later

Money is delayed feedback.

You do not feel the impact of skipping retirement contributions this year. You feel it decades later. You do not feel the impact of lifestyle creep immediately. You feel it when flexibility disappears. You do not feel the impact of ignoring insurance until something happens.

This delay is dangerous.

Athletes are conditioned to immediate feedback. A bad rep is corrected instantly. Money does not work that way. It allows mistakes to hide until recovery is harder.

This is why former athletes often say, "I wish I had known earlier."

They did know enough.

What they lacked was structure when no one was watching.

Golfers understand delayed consequences.

A poor tee shot might not hurt until the second shot. A bad decision early in the round shows up later. Financial decisions work the same way, just stretched over years instead of holes.

Game situations and decision points

Imagine this situation.

You receive a raise. No one tells you what to do with it. Do you upgrade lifestyle automatically, or do you capture the increase intentionally?

Another scenario.

You miss a month of saving. Do you ignore it and move on, or do you reset the system so it does not happen again?

A third scenario.

You feel financially fine right now. Do you assume that means you are on track, or do you verify through structure and review?

When no one is watching, these decisions define outcomes.

Common athlete mistakes and financial parallels

One common mistake is confusing freedom with lack of standards.

Freedom requires higher standards, not lower ones.

Another mistake is relying on motivation.

Motivation fades. Systems remain.

A third mistake is assuming future effort will fix current avoidance.

Later rarely fixes earlier without cost.

Athletes who succeed after sports replace external accountability with internal structure.

Winning the long game

The moment no one is watching is the moment the real game begins.

Not because it is harder physically, but because it demands ownership. Ownership of time. Ownership of habits. Ownership of money decisions that do not get applause.

Great golfers practice when no one is watching.

They build routines that carry them when pressure returns. Financial success requires the same quiet discipline.

When structure replaces accountability, consistency replaces intensity. When systems replace motivation, progress becomes automatic. When identity replaces pressure, discipline becomes durable.

Money mistakes do not happen all at once.

They happen quietly when no one is watching.

Build systems for those moments. Decide who you are without the crowd. Protect habits before they are tested.

That is how discipline survives freedom.

That is how the long game is actually won.

Athlete Takeaways

- Discipline without structure breaks down quietly
- Comfort feels earned but growth creates freedom
- Grind must evolve into systems and consistency
- Delayed feedback makes money mistakes harder to see
- Who you are when no one is watching determines everything

Chapter 29: Redefining Winning After the Uniform Comes Off

Every athlete eventually faces a quiet question.

If I am no longer measured by wins, stats, or playing time, how do I know if I am winning now?

When the uniform comes off, the scoreboard disappears. No box score. No rankings. No crowd reaction. That absence creates a vacuum. And vacuums get filled. For many former athletes, status replaces performance as the new measuring stick.

This chapter is about recognizing that shift, understanding why it happens, and intentionally redefining what winning actually looks like in adulthood.

Why chasing status replaces chasing performance

Sports give you clear metrics.

You know where you stand. You know how you are doing. Feedback is constant. When that structure ends, the human brain still craves validation. If performance metrics disappear, substitutes show up quickly.

Titles. Income. Houses. Cars. Lifestyle.

These become visible signals of success because they are easy to compare. They look like scoreboards. The problem is that they are poor measures of progress and terrible guides for decision-making.

Athletes are wired to compete.

If you do not define the game, you will compete in whatever game is loudest around you. In adulthood, that game is often status.

Status chasing feels productive.

You work harder. You earn more. You upgrade faster. But underneath, the motivation has changed. Instead of improving skill and execution, you are proving worth. That shift is exhausting and financially dangerous.

Golfers know this pattern.

Trying to outdrive everyone on the course rarely lowers scores. It just creates trouble. Winning requires discipline, not flash.

Income vs fulfillment

Income matters.

It provides stability, options, and security. Ignoring income is unrealistic. But income alone is not fulfillment, and confusing the two creates frustration.

Many former athletes reach income goals they once dreamed about and still feel unsettled. That discomfort is confusing if money was expected to be the answer.

Income measures output.

Fulfillment measures alignment.

Alignment between how you spend time, what you value, and who you are becoming. When those elements match, life feels steady even during challenges. When they do not, no amount of income fixes the tension.

Athletes understand this intuitively from sports.

There are seasons where playing time decreases but leadership grows. Where stats dip but impact increases. Fulfillment comes from contribution and growth, not just numbers.

Financially, fulfillment comes from clarity.

Knowing why you earn. Knowing what money is for. Knowing when enough is enough. Without that clarity, income becomes a moving target that never satisfies.

Titles, houses, cars, and comparison traps

Comparison is the most efficient way to lose direction.

Social media accelerates this problem. Everyone posts highlights. Promotions. Purchases. Vacations. The comparison trap convinces you that you are behind even when you are doing well.

Titles feel like validation.

They signal progress externally. But titles often say more about organizational structure than personal growth. Chasing titles without understanding role fit leads to burnout and instability.

Houses and cars are similar.

They are visible. They are praised. They create pressure to keep up. Overextending financially to match peers erodes flexibility quietly. Years later, the cost shows up as stress, not status.

Golfers avoid this trap by playing their own game.

They choose clubs based on distance, not on what others are swinging. Financial independence works the same way. Decisions should be based on goals and cash flow, not comparison.

Comparison shifts the game from winning to not losing.

That mindset creates fear-based decisions. Fear leads to forced shots. Forced shots lead to mistakes.

What "success" actually looks like in your 30s and 40s

Success evolves.

In your 20s, success often looks like opportunity and momentum. In your 30s and 40s, it looks more like stability, optionality, and control.

Control over time.

Control over commitments.

Control over stress.

Many former athletes realize later that success is being able to say no. To choose work intentionally. To invest in health. To be present with family. To handle setbacks without panic.

Financially, success looks like margin.

Margin in cash flow. Margin in savings. Margin in energy. Margin allows you to absorb surprises without blowing up your life.

It also looks like consistency.

Steady investing. Thoughtful career moves. Planned lifestyle growth. This is not flashy. It is effective.

Golfers mature into this understanding.

Early careers chase birdies. Later careers protect pars. Over time, pars win tournaments.

Building a new scoreboard

If you do not build a new scoreboard, the world will assign one to you.

That scoreboard will likely prioritize income, consumption, and appearance. Those metrics are easy to measure and easy to exploit.

A better scoreboard is personal.

Financial independence progress. Savings rate. Investment consistency. Debt reduction. Stress levels. Health markers. Time spent with people you care about. Alignment with values.

These metrics are quieter, but they matter more.

Building a new scoreboard requires honesty.

What actually matters to you now. Not what used to matter. Not what impresses others. What supports the life you want to live.

Athletes who succeed after sports take ownership of the game definition.

They decide what winning means. They track the right stats. They stop chasing noise.

Golfers who keep playing well into later life adjust expectations and metrics.

They still compete, but they compete against themselves and the course, not against everyone else's highlight reel.

Game situations and decision points

Imagine this situation.

You are offered a higher-paying role with longer hours and more stress. Do you take it automatically, or do you evaluate what it costs beyond income?

Another scenario.

Friends upgrade lifestyles rapidly. You feel behind. Do you follow, or do you stick to a plan aligned with your goals?

A third scenario.

You hit a financial milestone. Instead of feeling satisfied, you feel pressure to reach the next one. Do you pause and reassess, or do you keep chasing without clarity?

These moments define whether you are winning your game or someone else's.

Common athlete mistakes and financial parallels

One mistake is assuming success should feel the same forever.

It does not. Goals evolve.

Another mistake is equating visibility with value.

Quiet progress often matters more.

A third mistake is avoiding reflection.

Without reflection, growth becomes accidental.

Athletes who redefine winning intentionally transition more smoothly into long-term success.

Winning the long game

Redefining winning is not lowering standards.

It is choosing better ones.

When the uniform comes off, the game does not end. It changes. The skills that made you successful still matter. Discipline. Preparation. Patience. But the metrics shift.

Money becomes a tool, not a trophy.

Status becomes irrelevant. Alignment becomes central.

Great golfers know when to change strategy.

Great former athletes know when to change the scoreboard.

Define winning on your terms. Track what actually matters. Build a life that feels strong even when no one is clapping.

That is real success after sports.

Athlete Takeaways

- If you do not define winning, someone else will
- Status is loud, alignment is powerful
- Income supports life, it is not the scoreboard
- Comparison creates forced shots and bad decisions
- Build a scoreboard that measures freedom, not flash

Chapter 30: Staying Connected Without Living in the Past

Every former athlete knows the feeling.

You miss the locker room. The jokes. The shared grind. The feeling of belonging to something bigger than yourself. You do not necessarily miss the conditioning or the injuries. You miss the connection.

When the uniform comes off, that connection often disappears overnight.

This chapter is about learning how to stay connected without getting stuck, how to honor what sports gave you without letting it define you forever, and how to build a forward-looking identity that supports long-term success in life and money.

The role of community, mentorship, and new locker rooms

Sports provide built-in community.

You do not have to search for it. It is assigned. Teammates. Coaches. Staff. Shared goals create instant trust and shared language. That environment is rare outside sports.

When it disappears, many former athletes underestimate the impact.

They assume independence should feel empowering. Instead, isolation creeps in quietly. There is no group chat. No shared mission. No collective accountability. Life becomes individualized very quickly.

Community matters because it stabilizes behavior.

People around you influence habits, mindset, and expectations. Athletes surrounded by disciplined peers tend to stay disciplined. Athletes who drift into isolation often struggle to maintain routines.

New locker rooms do not appear automatically.

They must be built intentionally. Professional groups. Mentorship relationships. Faith communities. Fitness groups. Alumni networks. These spaces recreate connection without replicating the past.

Mentorship becomes especially important.

In sports, guidance is constant. In adulthood, mentorship replaces coaching. Mentors provide perspective, not instruction. They help you navigate ambiguity and see around corners.

Golfers often play their best rounds with people who challenge them quietly. Community works the same way in life.

Why isolation hits former athletes hard

Former athletes are conditioned to belong.

Your identity is reinforced daily. Your role is clear. When that reinforcement disappears, silence replaces structure. That silence can feel uncomfortable and unfamiliar.

Isolation affects decision-making.

Without peers who understand discipline, standards slip. Without shared language, struggles feel personal instead of normal. Without comparison to process, comparison shifts to outcomes.

Isolation also impacts money.

Spending increases to replace connection. Lifestyle upgrades become substitutes for belonging. Busy schedules replace purpose. These patterns are not character flaws. They are responses to disconnection.

Athletes who isolate often do so unintentionally.

They assume others will not understand their experience. They downplay their past. Or they cling to it too tightly. Both paths create distance.

Golfers struggle alone too.

Practicing without feedback eventually creates bad habits. Financial habits suffer the same way without community and accountability.

Finding purpose without the team

Purpose shifts after sports.

During competition, purpose is external. Win games. Support teammates. Execute roles. After sports, purpose must be internalized. That transition is difficult.

Many former athletes try to replace the team immediately.

They overwork. Overcommit. Overidentify with jobs. This creates short-term structure but long-term imbalance.

Purpose is not found in replacement teams.

It is found in contribution.

Teaching. Mentoring. Building. Leading. Creating. Purpose comes from impact, not applause. The scale may change, but the meaning does not have to.

Golfers experience this transition clearly.

Early on, competition drives purpose. Later, teaching the game, mentoring younger players, or simply playing well becomes enough. Financial life follows a similar arc.

Purpose anchors money decisions.

When you know why you are earning, saving, and investing, choices become easier. Without purpose, money becomes reactive. Reactive money creates stress.

Healthy nostalgia vs being stuck

Nostalgia is not the enemy.

Remembering great moments. Laughing about past trips. Honoring the journey. These memories matter. They shaped who you are.

The problem is living there.

Being stuck in the past often shows up subtly. Constant comparison to who you used to be. Measuring current life against peak moments. Talking about sports more than building the present.

This mindset limits growth.

You cannot move forward while constantly looking backward. Healthy nostalgia fuels gratitude. Being stuck fuels dissatisfaction.

Athletes stuck in the past often struggle financially too.

They delay planning. They chase status to recreate validation. They avoid long-term thinking because the future feels uncertain.

Golfers know that replaying old rounds does not improve the next one.

You learn from the past, then you move on. Financial and personal growth require the same discipline.

Creating a forward-looking identity

Identity drives behavior.

In sports, identity is given. Position. Team. Role. After sports, identity must be chosen. That freedom is powerful and uncomfortable.

A forward-looking identity focuses on who you are becoming, not who you were.

Builder. Professional. Parent. Mentor. Investor. Leader. These identities create direction. Direction supports consistent habits.

Financial decisions align more easily when identity is clear.

A builder saves to create. A mentor invests to give. A leader plans to protect others. Without identity, decisions become reactive and inconsistent.

Creating a new identity does not erase the old one.

It integrates it.

Discipline. Preparation. Resilience. Team-first mindset. These traits still apply. They are just expressed differently.

Golfers who age well do this beautifully.

They adapt their game. They adjust expectations. They find satisfaction in consistency and presence. Former athletes can do the same in life and money.

Game situations and decision points

Imagine this situation.

You feel disconnected and start spending more to feel better. Do you recognize the signal and rebuild connection, or do you keep masking the issue financially?

Another scenario.

You avoid new communities because they feel awkward. Do you retreat into the past, or do you lean into discomfort and build something new?

A third scenario.

You constantly compare current life to peak sports moments. Do you honor the past and move forward, or do you let comparison steal satisfaction?

These choices shape identity and outcomes.

Common athlete mistakes and life parallels

One mistake is assuming connection will happen naturally.

It rarely does after sports.

Another mistake is replacing team identity with work identity.

Work is part of life, not the locker room.

A third mistake is avoiding reflection.

Without reflection, nostalgia becomes a trap.

Athletes who thrive long term build community intentionally and redefine belonging.

Winning the long game

Staying connected without living in the past is a skill.

It requires intention. Humility. Willingness to be new at something again. The same courage it took to walk into a locker room as a freshman is required to build community after sports.

Financial success depends on this too.

Connected people make better decisions. They spend less to compensate.

They plan with perspective. They invest with patience.

You do not need to recreate the team.

You need to create connection.

Honor the past. Appreciate it. Then build forward. Create new locker rooms. Find mentors. Be a mentor. Define identity intentionally.

The uniform may come off, but belonging does not have to.

Athlete Takeaways

- Community stabilizes habits and decision-making
- Isolation quietly undermines discipline and money choices
- Purpose comes from contribution, not applause
- Nostalgia is healthy until it replaces growth
- Forward-looking identity creates consistent progress

Disclaimers

Educational Purpose Only

This book is for educational purposes only.

The information provided in *GolfMoney101* is intended to help readers understand general financial concepts using golf-based analogies. It is not individualized financial, investment, tax, legal, or insurance advice.

Every financial situation is different. Your goals, income, family circumstances, risk tolerance, and time horizon are unique. What works for one person may not be appropriate for another.

Not Financial, Investment, or Legal Advice

Nothing in this book should be interpreted as a recommendation to buy, sell, or hold any specific investment, financial product, or strategy.

This book does not replace advice from qualified professionals such as:

- Financial advisors
- Accountants or tax professionals
- Attorneys
- Insurance professionals

Before making financial decisions, readers should consult professionals who can evaluate their individual situation and provide personalized guidance.

No Guarantees or Promises of Results

All investing involves risk, including the possible loss of principal.

Past performance does not guarantee future results. Markets fluctuate. Economic conditions change. Outcomes cannot be predicted or guaranteed.

The examples, scenarios, and illustrations in this book are for educational purposes only and may not reflect actual results or real-world outcomes.

Tax and Legal Information

Any discussion of taxes, retirement accounts, estate planning, or legal structures in this book is general in nature.

Tax laws and regulations change frequently and vary by jurisdiction. Legal requirements differ based on location and individual circumstances.

Readers should seek personalized tax or legal advice before acting on any information related to these topics.

Athlete and Career Considerations

This book discusses financial topics as they relate to athletes and former athletes, including career transitions, income variability, and life after competition.

It does not provide career placement services, employment advice, or guarantees related to income, compensation, endorsements, or career success.

Use of Analogies

Golf and sports analogies are used throughout this book to make financial concepts easier to understand.

These analogies are educational tools only and should not be interpreted literally. Financial decisions require analysis beyond analogy and should be based on facts, individual circumstances, and professional guidance when appropriate.

Personal Responsibility

By reading this book, you acknowledge that:

- You are responsible for your own financial decisions
- You understand that financial outcomes involve uncertainty
- You agree to seek appropriate professional guidance when needed

Education improves decision-making, but responsibility remains with the individual.

Contact Information

If you would like to learn more about the concepts discussed in this book or explore additional educational resources, Pat Brown can be found through public platforms including LinkedIn, Twitter, and via Google search.

For questions specifically related to *GolfMoney101*, you may contact Pat Brown at:

info@golfmoney101.com

Final Reminder

Financial success is built over time through discipline, planning, and consistency.

This book provides a framework, not a guarantee.

Use it as a guide, not a substitute for professional advice.

Glossary of Golf and Financial Terms

This glossary connects key financial concepts to familiar ideas from **golf**, making money easier to understand through the language, structure, and discipline golfers already know.

Asset Allocation

Financial Definition:

How money is divided among different investment types such as stocks, bonds, and cash to balance risk and return.

Golf Comparison:

Club selection and course strategy. You do not hit driver on every hole. Balance and shot selection keep you in position.

Assets

Financial Definition:

Things you own that have value, such as cash, investments, real estate, or retirement accounts.

Golf Comparison:

Your tools and skills. Swing fundamentals, course knowledge, short game, and experience that contribute to scoring.

Bonds

Financial Definition:

Loans made to governments or companies that pay interest and return principal over time.

Golf Comparison:

The safe play. Like laying up to the fat part of the fairway to stay in control.

Budget

Financial Definition:

A plan for how income is allocated toward expenses, savings, and goals.

Golf Comparison:

Your course management plan. Without a plan, every hole becomes reactive.

Cash Flow

Financial Definition:

Money coming in versus money going out.

Golf Comparison:

Energy management over 18 holes. Burn too much early and you struggle to finish.

Compounding

Financial Definition:

Earnings that generate additional earnings over time.

Golf Comparison:

Practice reps. Small improvements stack and lower scores over time.

Credit

Financial Definition:

The ability to borrow money with the promise of repayment.

Golf Comparison:

Reputation on the course. When trusted, you get opportunities. When abused, options disappear.

Debt

Financial Definition:

Money borrowed that must be repaid, often with interest.

Golf Comparison:

Carrying extra weight. Manageable in small amounts, harmful when excessive.

Diversification

Financial Definition:

Spreading investments across different assets to reduce risk.

Golf Comparison:

Having a full bag. You cannot play well with only one club.

Emergency Fund

Financial Definition:

Savings set aside for unexpected expenses.

Golf Comparison:

A recovery shot. You hope not to need it, but it saves the round when trouble shows up.

ETF (Exchange-Traded Fund)

Financial Definition:

A fund that holds many investments and trades like a stock.

Golf Comparison:

A well-designed course strategy instead of relying on one perfect swing.

Fees / Expense Ratios

Financial Definition:

Costs associated with managing investments.

Golf Comparison:

Poor course management. Small mistakes that quietly add strokes.

Growth Investing

Financial Definition:

Investing in companies expected to grow faster than average.

Golf Comparison:

Aggressive shot selection. Higher upside with more risk if fundamentals are weak.

Insurance

Financial Definition:

Protection against financial loss from unexpected events.

Golf Comparison:

Rain gear or proper spikes. You do not play unprotected when conditions turn.

Liquidity

Financial Definition:

How easily money can be accessed without penalty or delay.

Golf Comparison:

Shot options. Flexibility when conditions change mid-round.

Net Worth

Financial Definition:

Assets minus liabilities.

Golf Comparison:

Your total score. Not one hole, the entire round.

Rebalancing

Financial Definition:

Adjusting investments back to their intended mix over time.

Golf Comparison:

Making adjustments between holes to stay on plan.

Risk

Financial Definition:

The chance that outcomes differ from expectations, including loss.

Golf Comparison:

Shot difficulty. The tighter the line, the higher the reward and the danger.

Roth IRA

Financial Definition:

A retirement account where money grows tax-free if rules are followed.

Golf Comparison:

Putting in the work early so the finish is clean and stress-free.

Stocks

Financial Definition:

Ownership shares in a company.

Golf Comparison:

Drivers. Powerful tools that create distance but require control.

Tax-Advantaged Accounts

Financial Definition:

Accounts that provide tax benefits, often with rules and restrictions.

Golf Comparison:

Tournament rules. Restrictions exist to protect fairness and outcomes.

Volatility

Financial Definition:

Short-term ups and downs in market value.

Golf Comparison:

A bounce or bad lie. Normal unless you panic and force the next shot.

Permanent Loss

Financial Definition:

Money that cannot recover due to poor decisions or panic.

Golf Comparison:

A penalty stroke caused by abandoning fundamentals.

Total Return

Financial Definition:

Investment return from both price growth and income.

Golf Comparison:

Your full scorecard. Every hole counts.

Value Investing

Financial Definition:

Investing in assets believed to be undervalued.

Golf Comparison:

Smart course management. Less flash, more consistency.

Yield

Financial Definition:

Income generated from an investment.

Golf Comparison:

Pars. Not dramatic, but they win rounds over time.

Final Note

This glossary reinforces one core principle:

Financial success, like success in **golf**, comes from balance, discipline, timing, and repetition.

That philosophy runs through **GolfMoney101** and applies long after the round is over.

Pat Brown OLB, University of Kansas

Made in the USA
Monee, IL
04 November 2026

67386764R00115